Fit to Teach

Fit to Teach

A private inquiry into the training of teachers, with recommendations

Edited by Bruce Kemble

HUTCHINSON EDUCATIONAL

HUTCHINSON EDUCATIONAL LTD
3 Fitzroy Square, London W1

London Melbourne Sydney Auckland
Wellington Johannesburg Cape Town
and agencies throughout the world

First published 1971

*This book has been set in Bembo type, printed in Great Britain
on antique wove paper by Anchor Press, and
bound by Wm. Brendon, both of Tiptree, Essex*

ISBN 0 09 110311 8

Acknowledgements

I am deeply grateful to the following for their advice, help and encouragement:

Roger Beard, Roy Nash, the late Dr Stephen Wiseman, my wife Helen, who among other things typed the manuscript and made the late-night coffee, and my secretary, Jill Todd, who will be glad it is all over now.

Contents

Introduction

Lord Boyle

The question 'What makes a good teacher?' is just about the most important in education. During the past twelve years there has been an exceptionally rapid growth in the numbers of student teachers in colleges of education, as well as an increase in the length of their initial training course. Yet many students are still dissatisfied with what they are getting, and there has been far too little searching discussion of aim and content, or of those qualities which have enabled the best teachers, the best colleges and the best schools to develop a real partnership with home and local community.

The Plowden Report on primary education made some damaging criticism of the secondary school background of many students in training. 'Too many students,' the Report said, 'have concentrated in the sixth form on English, history and geography, too few are qualified to take college main courses in mathematics, science or music. The secondary schools with their specialist tradition are not sufficiently aware of the need of the primary schools for teachers whose value lies in a marked degree in their versatility.'

A worrying feature of British education today is the frequent isolation of our academic sixth forms, and our institutions of higher education, from the primary schools and from those secondary schools where 'Half our Future' is at stake. One of the finest civil servants I ever knew, Derek Morrell, used to say that it was always hard for a teacher who had benefited from a selective system of education to remember to ask himself, when teaching 'Newsom' children, 'What are the right goals for these children?' and *not* 'What are the goals that I should like to impose on them?'

There are a number of reasons why the question 'What makes a good teacher?' is particularly topical at the present time. First there is the imminence of the raising of the school-leaving age. No one doubts that the implementation of this long-delayed reform will bring problems, sometimes acute problems, for individual schools and for many individual teachers, but it will also bring important fresh opportunities. 'Secondary' education, as opposed to senior elementary education, cannot begin until the basic skills have been sufficiently mastered to enable boys and girls to acquire understanding of the uses to which those skills can be put, so that they become actively engaged in their own education; this is why both the Crowther and the Newsom Committees took the view, in my opinion rightly, that the raising of the school-leaving age to 16 must be regarded as a test of our national commitment to the ideal of 'Secondary education for all'. Incidentally, I wonder how many of those who write to the press opposing this reform would have allowed *their* children to leave school at 15.

Secondly, there is the prospect of a very rapid growth of numbers in school sixth forms, from 260,000 in 1969 to nearly half a million by 1975. We cannot any longer be content with just making a token gesture towards the non-academic sixth-former; he needs a varied yet integrated provision, with opportunities for creative work. And he is one of the main reasons why we need to think about the in-service training of teachers—how, when and where this should be carried out (and at whose expense) —no less than about their actual training.

Thirdly, one important mark of current educational thinking is what Sir Alec Clegg has called, in a striking phrase, 'the redistribution of concern'. More and more people have been pressing the need for 'enriching resources', both human and material, to be diverted to those areas which, in default of compensatory action, are bound to be areas of social and educational deprivation. Teaching the socially deprived has been well described by Dr Eric Midwinter as at once the most tiring and most meaningful of educational tasks. . . . The single finest encouragement is the hundreds of teachers who manage it brilliantly.'

Lastly, there is the nation-wide discussion of teacher education. In this connection, I cannot imagine a better curtain-raiser than the admirable collection of papers on specific topics, all of them both readable and informative, which Bruce Kemble has assembled in this volume *Fit to Teach*. I have already quoted from Dr Midwinter's contribution, and there are many others, for instance Mr Bourne's, which strike me as equally valuable. Mr Bourne mentions the problem of inadequate libraries in the colleges of education, and also the complaint that the staff 'do not do enough research'. On the first of these two points I'm sure he is right, and inequalities of library provision seem to be among the most indefensible inequalities within higher education today. The second point raises the difficult and important question, far too often overlooked in discussions of the 'binary system', of just what kinds of research—and how much—the 'non-autonomous' (i.e. non-university) institutions of higher education ought to be undertaking. As I see it, it could be sensible for the colleges of education to try to replicate the research already being carried out in universities, and Mr Bourne himself rightly points out the damages of college courses becoming 'a pale reflection of what university departments were doing some years previously'. But there is surely much research that still needs to be done into the best means of synthesising the findings of a number of disciplines for the benefit of children, and I should personally like to see the colleges directly involved in this work, alongside university departments of education.

Readers of this book will find that the authors, as a group, have been very successful in their aim of capturing the 'coal-face reality' of the classroom. It is an exceptionally readable book, yet definitely not 'lightweight'. And while many of the chapters are highly disturbing, the final message is not one of despondency. We *do* know some of the answers to the question 'What makes a good teacher?' and our most urgent objective should be to establish the conditions under which the best existing practice can be spread more widely. Even more important, this book teaches the lesson that there is no inconsistency between, on the one hand, a belief in intellectual rigour, and on the other, the recognition of those essential values of human equality and human dignity which are integral to the ideal of a civilised society.

Edward Boyle

Foreword

Bruce Kemble

The gap between rhetoric and reality is rarely more obvious than in books about education. Practising teachers rightly reject much of our efforts because they bear little, or no relation to, as Michael Pollard often says, 'the smell of wet wellies on a Monday morning in November'. Evidence to decision-makers about teacher training is usually inadequate for this reason. The voice giving the evidence is mostly an administrator, or the articulate voice of the union politician. The voice is often heard by men and women who have not been in a classroom since the day they left school. How many members of the Select Committee which studied teacher training had actually taught?

The voice we need to heed is the voice of the classroom teacher. Any discussion of the question: 'What makes a good teacher?' must be related to the coal-face reality of the classroom. Today's teachers are the first people we should turn to when we want to find the answer to the question: 'Is the present training system producing the right sort of teachers?' They can spell out how the theory of their three-year college course failed to prepare them for the daily struggle to control, and communicate with, forty pupils in a draughty classroom. They can say whether the practice they were given was long, or varied, enough. They can tell us if our schools and colleges are failing *them*.

This book was Michael Pollard's idea. I have acted as the mid-wife. Richard Bourne was the third member of the trio who conceived and created the over-all structure of this inquiry. He inspired and co-ordinated our efforts to reach conclusions on the reforms needed. The final drafting of our recommendations was, however, master-minded by Nicholas Bagnall. That section of the book would have been impossible without him. Michael, Richard and I chose the subjects we wanted investigated first, and we then selected the most suitable available authors. When we needed an expert we were lucky that a man such as Professor Evans, or Gordon Pemberton, or Ron Deadman (with his 15 years' primary school experience) agreed to help us. When we needed a freelance journalist to spend time, and money, travelling around talking to teachers, we were fortunate that Frances Verrinder came to our aid.

Their efforts are full of the voices of classroom teachers. The chapters may not have totally captured the smell of the 'wellies', but they never let us forget for long that teaching 'is about the register as well as Plato', as Ron Deadman puts it. It comes as no surprise to read David Fletcher's chapter: 'On the day I spoke to her her arm was badly cut and bruised where a hysterical nine-year-old had dug in her finger-nails during a class-room tantrum.' By the time we get to John Ezard's chapter and read: 'Frankie Philips got stabbed outside his class once . . .', we realise how shocking it is that a study of 1,400 student teachers by Dr Donald Lomax could not find one student with experience of slum conditions. Training must prepare a teacher for the fact that he, or she, probably comes from a relatively secure, middle-class, suburban home, and the pupils are mostly working-class. Seven out of ten teachers are middle-class, and seven out of ten children are working-class. Every probe into training must take account of this central fact.

I am delighted that our contributors have remembered our urgings on this point. No doubt we have been guilty of jargon, and rhetoric, but it is never long before the concrete replaces the abstract. One example which gave me particular pleasure was the quotation in Michael Pollard's chapter: 'I take the car, but apparently my local authority doesn't believe in teachers riding in cars because all I can claim back is the bus fare. So I rush home at four o'clock and grab some tea, and off I go to the course. By the time it ends, and I've had a drink with the others, it's half-past eight, so I either have to buy a meal out, or have my supper heated up when I get home. I can't claim for a meal, of course; my local authority doesn't believe in teachers eating either, it seems. So I've missed my favourite TV programme, and I'll have to get to school early the next day to finish my marking—and for what? I suppose it's something to put on my application form, but that's about all.'

This teacher contrasts his re-training with the course available for a hot-metal compositor who got a productivity bonus for allowing the bosses to re-train him in their time!

We have tried to encourage our hard-pressed authors to link their chapters to reality in this way. We realise, however, that in any examination of the education, and training, of teachers it is necessary to study the academic side of the subject. We must not allow our interest in *practical* problems to obscure the fact that terms like 'The Philosophy of Education' do have a meaning.

An inquiry which attempts to draw attention to the depressing part of our education system is in danger of concentrating on negative aspects. We have attempted, therefore, in the longest of the three sections, to give as much positive help as possible from four experts on the problems of teaching numeracy, literacy, tough pupils, and children from a different background.

We hope the teaching staff in the colleges of education will find our effort as readable as the students it is designed to help.

Part I

Who are our teachers?

1 Teachers and training
Nicholas Bagnall

'The Committee was impressed with the co-operative attitude of the students, their ability to express themselves cogently and their obvious concern about questions of the content and methods of education employed in the education courses. . . . We were pleased to find a generation of students who, instead of accepting whatever was offered without comment, were clearly involved in the educational issues which arose, and capable of criticising their courses constructively.'

That came from the report of a sub-committee of the University of Leicester School of Education as part of its Area Training Organisation's inquiry. But what about this one?

'Eventually half the sample arrived at college as a result of a process of complete drift. . . . When the students considered the whole curriculum, their general verdict was that they were only moderately interested. . . . Most members of staff were unaware of this situation.'

That was from Donald Lomax's sample survey[1] of students at a college of education near Manchester. Which is nearer the truth? One can hardly assume that all the good 'uns go to Leicester, and the bad 'uns to Manchester.

Dr John McLeish,[2] when he was at the Cambridge Institute of Education, took a microscopic view of more than 1,200 students in ten colleges in the Cambridge area, and found the intake 'surprisingly conservative and establishment-minded'. Sixty per cent said they were effective members of the Church of

[1] For references, see p. 33

England, and 44 per cent declared themselves to be Tory compared with 16 per cent Labour. Only 15 per cent said they had no religion. This doesn't mean that the colleges recruit mainly from the well-to-do suburbs, where such views are supposed to predominate. The Robbins Report of 1963 showed 52 per cent of men teacher trainees coming from manual backgrounds, and 42 per cent of the women.* These are far higher figures than those for the universities. William Taylor,[3] in *Society and the Education of Teachers*, considers this may help to account for the resistance that has been noted to the discussion of social class in college of education courses. One is reminded of the story of the principal of a small college who exclaimed that she was not going to have her girls troubled with all this talk about class, when confronted with a proposed sociology syllabus. Taylor notes that, although there is a fair proportion of working-class students in the colleges, the colleges themselves do not interest themselves much in political or industrial matters; moreover, in the 'teacher-education culture', as he calls it, 'intellect is regarded with a certain amount of suspicion'. Instead, discussion tends to concentrate on peripheral social issues such as pollution or the effects of the advertising industry on the quality of society.

Trainee teachers have a tendency to turn their backs on the kind of issue which might be expected to interest industrial workers, although a large proportion of them are the sons and daughters of industrial workers. This is not entirely surprising, when you remember that 74 per cent of the men in the Robbins sample and 69 per cent of the women had been to maintained grammar schools, one of whose aims is to 'declass' their pupils. The inference from both Lomax and Taylor is that the colleges aren't doing their job if part of that job is to give students an understanding of the culture of those they are being trained to teach. Professor G. H. Bantock (incidentally a professor at Leicester, from whence comes the quotation at the start of this

* Lomax's sample broke up thus: 30 per cent professional or managerial, 30 per cent lower professional or clerical, 30 per cent supervisory or skilled manual, 10 per cent self-employed or semi-skilled. 'No student could be found who had any experience of slum conditions.'

chapter) told the Select Committee on teacher training[4]: 'On occasions I have had students, to whom I have been giving orals, frankly telling me that they regarded some of their colleagues—and indeed, from my experience of interviewing some of them, I would tend to agree with this—as being intellectually dead, intellectually not stimulating. . . . I must say I go away from a number of colleges feeling a little depressed at the lack of sheer intellectual stimulation which I get from the students.'

So far, then, Lomax seems to be winning on points. A picture begins to emerge of stagnant-minded and conformist students in stagnant and conformist colleges. The National Foundation for Educational Research, in a note to the Select Committee,[5] was disturbed by 'the apparent lack of any signs of significant curriculum development in the colleges themselves'. The note goes on: 'The basic structure of the college course has changed little since the war. Even the introduction of the three-year course—an obvious opportunity for radical revision—seemed to result merely in the re-crystallisation of the former pattern, in spite of the many discussions and controversies which preceded the change.'

Many colleges—probably most—would say this was quite unfair. The evidence to the Select Committee is full of protestations to the contrary. However, large tracts of that evidence consisted of opinion rather than hard fact. Let's look at some more research.

The John McLeish work which I have already mentioned is among the most painstaking. His almost obsessively detailed analysis of the characters of more than 1,200 students, first at the beginning, then at the end of their three-year courses, showed that the colleges do have an influence on their students, and quite a marked one. They are not quite as ineffectual as some of the quotations above might make you imagine. McLeish found that on being retested after three years the students' personalities had not changed, which he regards as a bit odd in view of the belief of many lecturers that 'personality is the key to effective teaching'. A somewhat daunting conclusion. What he did find, though, was what he calls 'an increase in social radicalism'. The expression is part of educational psychologist's armoury of terms used in personality inventories. But down the page McLeish becomes plainer: 'They are significantly less favourable to physical punishment in schools, in general; they are more against formal methods of instruction and class organisation; they believe more in spontaneous development in children (Rousseau-istic "naturalism") and they are more tough-minded.' They also tend to have become less religious, in the formal sense.

Moreover, these changes are not, says the careful McLeish, simply the result of a natural growing up. (He tried the same questions on student nurses.) They are distinctly related to the kind of college the students went to. The changes, in short, were bigger among students in the 'better' colleges, 'better' being defined not in terms of 'progressive', but simply in terms of their amenities and environment (libraries, well-qualified staff, concern for individuality, intellectual climate and so forth).

One is tempted to react to all this by asking why, in that case, the teaching profession isn't changing more rapidly than it is—after all, half the profession is under 35 and the proportion of students to teachers is about one in three. Surely the changes found in these students must sooner or later be reflected among the staffs of schools? Yet the impression given by a fair body of research is that teachers remain conservative and resistant to change.

More, admittedly very much less extensive, research, written up in 1965 by D. S. Finlayson and Louis Cohen,[6] and published two years later in the *British Journal of Educational Psychology*, throws some quite fascinating light on this paradox.

The authors looked at the college careers of 268 women teachers in an effort to find out what they thought a teacher's rôle was. They used a long list of questions to elicit this; 72 per cent of the answers showed no significant change between the students' first and third years in college. The highly dispiriting conclusion seemed to be that 'teachers in training do not acquire growing insight into the teacher's rôle'. But, if this was so, it was not for lack of the colleges' trying. Finlayson and Cohen found 'a high peak of understanding and insight' *in the second year of the course.* It was in that year that the students were showing less authoritarian attitudes towards their pupils, and 'more regard for practices and beliefs concerned with the mental health and emotional well-being of the children'. Then in the third year these trends gave way to ideas not unlike those which the students had had in their *first* year—'which they gained, no doubt', comment the authors, 'from being pupils at school'. The second year was the year of 'maximum liberality'. During that year there was the biggest difference between the students' and the head teachers' views of the teachers' rôle, judging by questions the authors also put to 183 primary and secondary heads. The heads' answers 'go beyond the mean responses of students towards a relatively organisationally-oriented, child-dominating and conformity-desiring point of view'.

It could be, muse the authors, that the 'regression' in the third year may be the result of the students' growing awareness of the fact that they and the heads are apart from each other, and that they are anxious to narrow the gap. We thus seem to have a picture of the students caught in the shades of two prison-houses, the classroom they were taught in, and the classroom in which they are destined to teach, with a brief day of enlightenment in between.

All through the course there were differences in attitudes between the heads and the students—towards caning, sex education, school councils, pupils' dress and behaviour—the students being more liberal, the heads less. But *both* agreed in putting 'helping children to acquire correct manners and speech' high on their lists of things which a teacher must do: above the three Rs, in fact. 'Inculcating values not fostered in the home' also came high on both lists.

Frank Musgrove and P. H. Taylor,[7] writing in the same journal in 1965, had come to conclusions rather different from these, and in some ways more like McLeish's: they noted that among 740 teachers they questioned there was an increasing tendency to think of the teacher's rôle as being like that of the social worker rather than the instructor. These teachers put moral training and instruction higher on their list of aims than questions of dress and behaviour. But Musgrove and Taylor were asking questions about teachers' aims, rather than their preoccupations, and comparison with the Finlayson-Cohen research is hazardous.

The really interesting point about the Musgrove-Taylor paper is its examination of what teachers *thought* parents wanted, compared with what parents (237 of them were questioned) actually wanted themselves. The disparity turned out to be almost incredible, and makes one wonder whether any teachers have actually *met* a parent. (For example, most teachers thought parents rated 'social advancement' high for their children; actually they rated it second to bottom out of six items. Grammar school women teachers thought 'moral training' most important, guessed that parents put it fifth; actually parents put it first. And so forth.)

From such research we get a distinct impression of teachers as more than a little old-fashioned, and out of touch, and of colleges as lacking the influence, or the expertise, or the plain fizz, to alter the situation.

Elizabeth Goodacre,[8] in *School and Home* (N.F.E.R., 1970), quotes a research project by Nick Georgiades[9] showing that a sample of 240 teachers and trainees 'compared unfavourably with business managers in training courses when confronted by new ideas'. Her own large-scale investigation[10] among 100 London infant schools or departments led her to conclude, of teachers in lower-working-class areas, 'that their own language system and academically biased education might make it extremely difficult for many of them to recognise unfamiliar forms of intellectual functioning.' She noted that more teachers in these areas tended to accept that they had no pupils of above-average ability. Teachers' assessments showed that lower-working-class children were 'significantly inferior' in attainment; it is possible, she concludes, that teachers of working-class origin in lower-working-class schools underestimate their pupils' ability because of their 'status anxiety', and that middle-class teachers make the same mistake 'because they are unfamiliar with such children and their level of achievement'. She found that there was one particular reading scheme which was popular in all areas, irrespective of the pupils' social background, and of 'the environmental experiences the pupils might bring to the reading situation'.

She writes: 'Often in referring to the work of individual pupils a teacher would comment: "She should be able to do better, she comes from a good home", or, conversely: "What can you expect, he comes from a poor home".'

It is only fair to add that the situation may have improved since the Goodacre research since more colleges have begun to take the sociology of education more seriously. There is room, too, for disagreement about the importance of 'sympathetic' social attitudes among teachers. The point was well made in a leader in *Teacher's World*.[11] 'What should be asked,' it said, 'is: "Is it better, in the long run, for the children of manual workers to be faced with a middle-class teacher who feels it is his duty to use language which helps his slower learners to develop their intelligence? Or with a teacher who is so sympathetic to their plight that he rejects these techniques in the belief that they are alienating and semi-authoritarian?"'

If class is a contentious subject, there are plenty of other, less subjective, reasons for thinking that the colleges have failed. Brian Cane and Colin Schroeder[12] of the N.F.E.R. questioned more than 1,000 teachers from 147 schools to discover their attitudes towards research, and interviewed 165 of them. The only two authors who were familiar to the majority of 915 assistant teachers were Burt and Piaget; the majority of primary, but not secondary, assistants knew about the work of Dienes. All the other authors mentioned were *totally unknown* to between 53 and 97 per cent of the sample, according to which area they came from. The authors included John Downing, J. W. B. Douglas, Basil Bernstein, A. H. Halsey, Stephen Wiseman. . . . The interviews suggest that this sample of teachers at any rate are hardly voracious readers. 'I would appreciate,' said one, 'a way in which I could be made aware of what is going on without actually having to sit down (and read journals).'

One begins to understand what Taylor means when he says colleges are anti-intellectual. One of the witnesses for the National Association of Head Teachers[13] told the Select Committee: 'Some of the so-called cleverest men, they wrote books and so on, could not teach boys.' The remark is certainly true; the *way* it is put betrays straight Philistinism. (I don't mind picking this man out since he obviously won't be among those who read this book!)

Turning from literacy to numeracy, we find things rather worse, at least among the women. The classic source here is F. W. Land's *Recruits to Teaching*,[14] published by the University of Liverpool in 1960. He found 'gross ignorance of the simplest arithmetical facts' among a sample of 1,880 women trainees. Of the 884 who had no O level in maths, one-third were not up to the level which might be expected of some of the brighter children still in junior school.

The colleges are thus handicapped in the teaching of maths method from the start. In the teaching of reading there have been accusations that many don't really try: see Dr Joyce Morris's[15] evidence to the Select Committee, or that of the N.F.E.R.,[16] which points out, as Dr Morris does, that colleges mainly confine the teaching of reading to intending infant teachers. The N.F.E.R. partly blames the hallowed division between education lecturers and subject lecturers: college lecturers in English seem by and large to be teachers of English literature, neglecting language and leaving it to overworked education staff. The National Union of Teachers' Young Teachers' Advisory Committee[17] in 1969 did a survey among 246 teachers with less than five years' experience and found that, of the infant and junior teachers, 29 per cent had been inadequately taught in the teaching of reading and 17 per cent had not been taught at all. The picture may not be as bad as the N.F.E.R. evidence makes it sound, but it is not good.

The colleges are falling down even on the simplest and most obvious measures of success. The dissatisfactions of the students themselves have been well documented, as Richard Bourne's chapter very clearly shows, notably in successive surveys by the National Union of Students, by the National Union of Teachers, and, more meticulously, by the Bristol School of Education,[18] which concerned itself with the entire 1966 intake into the profession. The Bristol researchers found that the biggest difficulty young teachers had to cope with was that of teaching a wide range of ability. They were also worried about being unfamiliar with their pupils' social backgrounds.

More than 2,500 heads were questioned about probationers' difficulties, and six out of ten mentioned 'classroom discipline'. Forty per cent also mentioned unfamiliarity with social backgrounds, and 60 per cent lack of self-confidence. Forty-one per cent thought the probationers had 'inadequate organising ability'. The survey revealed a surprising lack of interest among local education authorities in the probationers' college reports when choosing, or placing, their new teachers. The majority were more interested in teaching-practice grades.

The shortcomings of teaching practice are mentioned time and time again by students and young teachers in questionnaires. It is too short, there is not enough of it, it is perfunctorily supervised or assessed; or, sometimes, it is 'artificial'; or, again, if it is term-long, it is exhausting nervously and physically for students still having to keep up their reading. Other complaints most often voiced include many about the course's lack of practical value, and some about the boredom of education lectures.

The majority are satisfied, in general, with the course; the Bristol survey came up with figures showing 64 per cent of third-term probationers looking back at their training as 'reasonably adequate', and eight per cent as entirely so. But one in four thought it had been 'barely adequate', or worse.

A survey done by Kent Education Committee[19] (undated, but apparently in 1964) asked more than 200 head teachers whether they had noticed any improvement in the all-round quality of the teachers produced by the three-year course compared with the two-year course. Only 29 of them gave an unqualified 'yes'. As many as 115 of them thought too little time was being spent on subjects related to practical teaching, and 48 thought too much time was spent on academic subjects.

There are limits, of course, to this kind of self-diagnosis, whether in teaching or in any other profession. The teachers who didn't like their training courses may have expected too much from them, or the heads may have themselves got a wrong notion of what to expect from their products. Conversely, the satisfied ones may be merely unimaginative or complacent. There are obvious limits, too, to the chances of a successful self-cure, though there has been no lack of prescriptions. The simplest prescription is the one which says: 'The trouble with the teaching profession is that it is not good enough because the standards of entry into the colleges are too low. Put up the standards, you'll get a better class of student, and hey, presto. But of course there's no point in putting up the standards unless you can be sure that the better class of student actually *wants* to go into a college of education. So you'll have to offer him a degree at the end of it all.' This is the basic mixture proposed by, among others, the National Union of Teachers[20] and the Association of Teachers in Colleges and Departments of Education, both of which are worried—and with good reason—about whether the colleges are going to get their fair share of sixth-form talent in the future.

The A.T.C.D.E.[21] points out with some alarm that although the academic mixture going into the colleges is much as before, the proportion of *available* A-levellers is declining. (Sixty-five per cent of the entrants had one or more As, and 37 per cent had two or more.) 'The colleges,' says the A.T.C.D.E., 'no longer draw their entrants from the ablest 16 per cent (in terms of attainment) of the population as they did in 1961. In 1961–2, 15·4 per cent of the relevant age group obtained five or more O-level passes; in 1971–2 it is estimated that 15·7 per cent will obtain two or more A-level passes . . .' And it goes on to say that the low entrance qualifications seem to be deterring able sixth-formers. The 1971 clearing-house figures show that the colleges wanted 39,000 entrants, but could accept only 37,384.

The colleges and the schools are probably right to feel uneasy. There is no doubt that a low general opinion of the profession does put some good young people off. The Economist Intelligence Unit,[22] working for the A.T.C.D.E., asked sixth-formers in 21 schools what they thought about teaching as a career. They spoke of poor pay, disciplinary problems, and the repetitive nature of the work. One in four said they were going into teaching, but many more said they *would* have done but for the poor pay. Incidentally, they were hopelessly misinformed: most thought teachers' initial pay compared badly with that in other professions, but more favourably later, whereas the reverse is the case. We can perhaps blame the N.U.T. for that.

The poor notion of teachers is not confined to schoolboys. The Registrar-General also appears to take a pretty dim view of them. R. K. and H. M. Kelsall[23] point out that in his Social Classes and Socio-Economic Groups assistant teachers are dumped in class 5, which is labelled 'Intermediate non-manual workers'. In 1970 the Assistant Masters' Association[24] asked more than 1,300 university undergraduates what they thought of the profession. Characteristic replies of those who had decided against teaching included: 'One gets the impression that teaching attracts the dedicated or aimless, but never the ambitious.'—'Seems to be the ideal career for those who cannot bolster their personalities sufficiently to leave the education system.'—'There is not much wrong with teaching, a lot wrong with teachers.'—'I shall not go into teaching largely because of the character and attitude of mind of most teachers—I do not want to be like them.'

It would be wrong to think that most students who do go to colleges of education are there as a sort of act of despair, because they can't get in anywhere else. The Bristol survey knocks this myth on the head by showing that 72 per cent of the sample had made teaching their first choice; among the graduates, the proportion was higher. The N.U.S. survey of 1971[25] asked more than 10,000 college of education students why they were there. Fewer than 2,000 said it was either because they couldn't find anywhere else, or from a 'desire to follow a course of higher education'. The rest said: 'Desire to teach.' The London Institute of Education inquiry got even more enthusiastic answers.

Among those who do go, there is often disillusionment. Lomax may have overstated the case when he wrote of 'drifters', but the lack of intellectual stimulation about which Bantock spoke remains. Anne Sutherland[26] at Aberdeen University devised a scale for measuring what students think of their colleges, based on the American College Characteristics Index. Students had to look at a huge battery of statements about their colleges, and say whether they were true or not. In an interim report she writes:

'At each college, the mean scores of the entrants and the experienced students were compared. The results suggest that new students who arrive at college expecting Utopia Unlimited turn into disillusioned and jaded seniors.' At one college, experienced students gave scores for 'intellectual demands' and 'cultural interests' which were less than half what the new entrants gave. The author comments: 'Admittedly many students arrive with quite unrealistic expectations, but need the reality be as uninspiring as some of them describe it approximately two years later?'

The obvious point here is that if you raise the entry standard, hoping to get livelier people, you may find *more* disillusionment still, not less—unless you change the syllabus, and, indeed, the entire climate of many of the colleges. The most significant attempt to do this has been the institution of the B.Ed. degree, which has disappointed the N.U.T. to such an extent that it has decided not to support it in its present form. There have been complaints that colleges have pampered the B.Ed. people to the neglect of the others, and that it is too theoretical, irrelevant or academic. (See particularly T. W. Eason's *Colleges of Education: Academic or Professional?*[27], the fruits of a wide survey among college principals.)

The trouble with the 'raise the standards' prescription is that we have only the rockiest idea of the criteria on which the standards ought to be based. There is no guarantee that conventional school examinations are the right measure of what the colleges want. (One is reminded of Liam Hudson's work[28] on convergent and divergent thinkers; G.C.E. syllabuses tend to encourage the former, whereas it may well be that what the colleges need is more of the latter.) The same is even true of college assessments. Various attempts have been made to define an accurate criterion, or range of criteria, for success in teaching, but without much luck. Stephen Wiseman and Brian Start,[29] later at the N.F.E.R., did a lot of work on it when they were at Manchester; some of it is summarised in the *British Journal of Educational Psychology*. Following up nearly 250 teachers five years after their training, they found little correlation between what their heads thought of them and the grades they got at college; moreover, college grades did not seem to relate much with their actual progress in the profession, measured by posts of responsibility and so forth. 'It may be', say the authors, 'that the colleges and the headmasters are using different criteria.' There was some agreement between them about the not-so-good teachers, but this was hardly helpful: what is needed is a measure of *success*. Not that a single measure is ever likely to be found; that would be too much to expect. As it is, unhappily, there seems to be no clear agreement about what the colleges are supposed to be doing, with the result that they try to do everything.

Prescriptions for a cure can generally be divided into two kinds. First, the kind which aims to raise standards, but often with little attention to the relationship between 'standard' and 'quality'— there has been a general assumption that one leads to the other. Second is the kind which tries to relate what is done in the colleges more closely with what is done in the schools. In the first category comes the A.T.C.D.E.'s proposal for liberal arts colleges, or something like them, getting away from the too early commitment, and giving B.A.s and B.Ed.s a common foundation course. The N.U.T.'s proposal of 'comprehensive universities' comes into this category, too. In the second category we find a whole range of suggestions. We have an increasing recognition (even among some area training organisations) that the academic 'main subject' should be more vocational; almost universal agreement that teachers should play a bigger part in training new entrants; proposals for exchanges of job between teachers and lecturers; and a number of organisational ideas such as sandwich-type courses or 'end-on' courses (on, say, the academic-plus-practical-plus-education-theory pattern, in that order.) And we have a compelling plea for a genuinely vocational, academically respectable degree course in education of the kind which might be approved by the C.N.A.A. in polytechnics.[30]

You can easily see that some of the ideas in the second category conflict with some in the first. The biggest area of agreement, meanwhile, is over the need to marry theory more closely with practice, and the idea of 'teacher-tutors' has been very widely

canvassed. To judge by some of the above reaserch it's not going
to be an easy marriage. But then nothing in this field is easy.
The Society for the Promotion of Educational Reform through
Teacher Training (S.P.E.R.T.T.T.) said in its evidence to James:
'We feel that any reform being recommended should be seen to
be directed primarily at improving the situation in the schools
for the benefit first of the pupils. Only then should consideration
be given to the needs, apprehensions and aspirations of teachers,
lecturers or principals.' Quite so. But it is surely no good thinking
you can alter people's frames of mind simply by giving them
letters after their names or altering the hierarchies they serve.
Such changes can be quickly made: the real changes come much,
much later.

REFERENCES

1. Burgess, T. (Ed.) *Dear Lord James.* Penguin Books, 1971
2. 'Students' Attitudes and College Environments', Cambridge Institute of Education, 1970
3. Taylor, W. *Society and the Education of Teachers.* Faber, 1969
4. *Teacher Training*, Vol. 1: Full Committee, H.M.S.O. 182/1, 1970
5. *Ibid*
6. 'The Teacher's Rôle: a comparative study of the conceptions of College of Education students and head teachers', *British Journal of Educational Psychology*, Vol. xxxvii, 1967
7. 'Teachers' and Parents' Conception of the Teacher's Role', *Brit. Jrnl. Ed. Psych.*, Vol. xxv, 1965
8. Goodacre, E. 'School and Home: a review of developments in school and home relationships', N.F.E.R., 1970
9. *Times Educational Supplement*, February 2nd, 1968
10. 'Reading in Infant Classes', N.F.E.R., 1967; 'Teachers and their Pupils' Home Background', N.F.E.R., 1968. (Vols. 1 and 2 of *Teaching Beginners to Read*)
11. *Teacher's World*, March 26, 1971
12. 'The Teacher and Research', N.F.E.R., 1970
13. *Teacher Training*, Vol. 1
14. Land, F. W. *Recruits to Teaching*, University of Liverpool, 1960
15. *Teacher Training*, Vol. IV: sub-committee B, H.M.S.O. 182/IV, 1970
16. *Ibid*, Vol. 1
17. *The Future of Teacher Education*, N.U.T., 1969
18. Unpublished. But see also *Reports on Education*, No. 68, H.M.S.O., January, 1971
19. *The Three-Year Course of Teacher Training*, Kent County Council
20. See *The Reform of Teacher Education*, N.U.T., 1971.
21. A.T.C.D.E.'s. preliminary statement to James, February, 1971. See also its main evidence, *The Professional Education of Teachers*
22. *Remuneration of Young Teachers: Effect on Recruitment Wastage*, A.T.C.D.E., 1970
23. Kelsall, R. K. and Helen M. *The School Teacher in England and the United States: The findings of empirical research*, Pergamon, 1969
24. *The Undergraduate View of Teaching*, A.M.A., 1970
25. *N.U.S. Survey of Student Teachers' Opinion*, N.U.S., 1971
26. Unpublished

B

27. Eason, T. W. 'The Principals and their Colleges', Part One of *Colleges of Education: Academic or Professional?* W. R. Niblett (Ed.), N.F.E.R., 1970

28. In, for example, *Contrary Imaginations*, Methuen, 1966

29. 'A Follow-up of Teachers Five Years after Completing their Training', *Brit. Jrnl. Ed. Psych.*, Vol. xxxv, November, 1965

30. See E. E. Robinson in *Dear Lord James*

Note This is not a bibliography or reading list, but a list of books or pamphlets directly referred to in the chapter. For a wider list see *Teacher Training* (Vol. 1 of the Select Committee evidence), pp. 253–6

2 Why be a teacher?

Alex Evans

The moment for putting the question arrives. Weeks ago the student completed the Clearing House forms stating his name, age, address, school, number of O- and A-levels taken or to be taken, whether or not he is a prefect and what his interests are. He is being interviewed for a place at a college of education, his first, second or even his third choice, and perhaps, even, his third interview. 'They' have gone through his form with him: they have questioned him about his youth club, his stamp collection, the good books he has read recently. And then: 'Now tell us, why do you want to be a teacher?'

He knew this was coming and he has the answer ready which he thinks will please them. It varies a little from applicant to applicant but it's a curiously difficult question to answer and it's best to be vaguely idealistic. 'Well, I'm fond of children', 'I think teaching children is a very important and worthwhile job', 'I always wanted to teach ever since I first attended the infant/junior/secondary school'. Interviewers may smile at the regularity with which these answers are trotted out, but who, after all, keeps on asking it? And isn't it a fair question?

There may, of course, be other reasons. A naïve applicant may reply that he had been advised to apply by his careers master (who may have thought this an easy way out when advising such a worthy and solid prefect who would never get to a university anyway). Another, rather quaint, reply is that 'I want to pass on the knowledge I have learnt at school to other children'—a strange motive when one considers the kind of knowledge he has acquired and the even more questionable idea that other children might want it and want to be crammed with it by him.

But however honest he may be, he should avoid the answer that he wants to be a teacher because of the long holidays. This is a very sensitive point with teachers and college lecturers, who, after all, were and still are teachers and have even longer holidays than their classroom colleagues. No one, of course, ever says that he wants to be a teacher because of the lovely lolly. 'I realise, of course,' says a very serious young man, 'that a teacher doesn't earn very much, but there is more to life than money' (and this at 18 plus, although, of course, he doesn't realise that quite a lot of teachers earn quite reasonable salaries). An answer which once delighted me came from an older man who said, 'But you don't seem to realise that I am earning more now than I shall ever earn as a teacher!' He now has a university job and gets good royalties on his books. Idealism sometimes pays.

It really is difficult to get any precise answer as to why people want to take up teaching. Is there a morbid and obsessive interest in the profession that makes people ask it more insistently of those who take it up than of those who go in for other professions like medicine, dentistry, electrical engineering or catering? What about 'vocation'? If, as the *Shorter Oxford* says, vocation is 'divine influence or guidance towards a definite career; the fact of being so-called or directed towards a special work in life; natural tendency to or fitness for such work', and if vocation is essential for entry to teaching, then we can cut recruitment by at least half.

And having a 'vocation', or being inspired by a marvellous teacher, or wanting to teach because it is the only way of making the world a better place to live in (that grand illusion) are not motives which *per se* make people good teachers. Indeed many people who enter teaching with such motives often find the initial shocks quite difficult to get over. Their vocational halo is not always distinguishable to children, quite a number of whom resist being done good to.

The question was easier to answer in the 19th and the early 20th century, for teaching was the chief way for intelligent boys and girls of the artisan classes to higher education, to better themselves by getting into the professional classes, albeit at a low level, into a white-collared job with a regular salary and security of tenure. Indeed, they were helped to rise by getting grants, two years for a training college and four for a degree and a training year. Our red-brick universities could hardly have survived without a plentiful supply of undergraduates on a Board of Education grant and a pledge to go in for teaching.

For over a hundred years teaching was the chief means of social advancement for intelligent working-class children, and although higher education and professional careers are now, in principle, open to all the talents, irrespective of class and income, it still holds good that a high proportion of the applicants for places in colleges of education are from the children of the artisan classes, first-generation grammar school children seeking the safe way up and, for the most part, not quite bright enough academically to obtain places in the universities and thus be free to delay the choice of career.

For what happens in our secondary schools today? Our in-increasingly large sixth forms consist of boys and girls mostly of 16 plus, adding O-level to their fifth-form scores and taking one to three A-levels. Those with a reasonable chance of high marks at A-level and the right grouping of subjects set their sights for the universities, often in the hope of getting an education and a qualification for some specific profession, but very often in the hope of obtaining an 'open' qualification such as an Arts degree or a B.Sc. in a 'pure' science, which will enable them to leave their options open in the first two and a half years. Many of these people, of course, go in for teaching when they fail to get those interesting jobs for which they fondly thought a first degree was the passport. 'I suppose I shall have to go in for teaching' is the sad farewell of so many graduates to the dreaming spires of Red-brick.

What about the non-university sixth-formers? In our highly competitive educational system these tend to be regarded as the also-rans. But reluctant to have their education terminated by an office or counter job and aspiring to a job with security and human contacts, many look to the colleges of education as the solution. Just as their pre-war counterparts in the sixth forms signed up for four years at the university and a teaching job afterwards because it was the only way they had of getting a university education, so the next echelon down signs on for three or four years of higher education in a college of education, knowing also that there is no law than can compel them to take up teaching or pay their money back.

They hear from their college friends (who do not know what the drop-out rate is) that the college course is a piece of cake and that if you keep your nose clean you are bound to pass. And, sadly, there is still some truth in this, for, with the long years of teacher-shortage still dinning in their ears, the colleges are reluctant to fail students who come up to their finals, particularly with all the sea-lawyers and discipline committees ready to pounce.

In spite of the criticism, much of it ill-informed, about the education and training of teachers the colleges of education are doing as good a job as they are allowed to do within the financial, professional, and social restrictions which still inhibit their development. It is greatly to their credit that the majority of young people who go to them develop an enthusiasm and even a sense of dedication to the job of education before they leave college. Their own education gives them something of a personal fulfilment, their professional work and their teaching practices a real and practical sense of purpose. Over the last ten years or so I myself have seen hundreds of students on their final teaching practice in schools all over the country, and it would be wrong of me not to pay tribute to them and the colleges which have trained them for their general professional competence, sincerity and conscientiousness.

All the same, many of these students have to get over a sense of personal inferiority, not only in the college but also in the schools where they find themselves working with trained and untrained graduates who are earning more—and who often jump ahead of them in their careers without necessarily being better teachers. Their resentments are sometimes expressed in their college newspapers and in the educational press. Many of them, particularly the men, resent having had to sign on for teaching as a condition of receiving higher education and resent that, unlike their university counterparts, they are on an also-ran course for an also-ran qualification of limited currency.

They find graduates, trained and untrained, getting the prestige jobs. They are administered by administrators, advised by advisors and inspected by inspectors, many of whom have not had the same length or type of experience as themselves. To compensate, they criticise their training and those in power over them. What profession is so ready to soil its own linen and wash it in public as the teachers? What other profession tells the public that it has been badly trained? Why do so many of the more resourceful, intelligent or energetic try to get out of the classroom into other branches of education? Why are the Mr Chipses regarded as such charming but pathetic creatures when they ought to be the most honoured?

This curious idea of having a vocation has always been a strong support for commitment at 18, although it is unrealistic and high-falutin to pretend that many people of that age—or indeed of any age—should be so compulsively inspired. And yet none of us has ever been able to state, clearly and precisely, what are the personal, emotional, sympathetic and intellectual qualities which distinguish the gifted teacher from the pedestrian. These qualities cannot be trained into him by the college, although, it must be asserted, the good teacher enjoys and gets far more out of his training than does the pedestrian and inadequate. The number of students who are good in the classroom and weak on theory is very small indeed.

The fact is that most reasonably intelligent people who can profit from higher education, like children, and enjoy a teaching situation are trainable as teachers. All the more important, then, that when they decide to take it on they should be trained and that their training should be such that they are constantly open to the impact of new discoveries about learning and new techniques in teaching.

It is interesting that recruitment to teaching has not previously been affected, quantitatively, by the inadequacy of the financial award. Although better off than an artisan in the 19th century, the teacher with his house and £60–90 p.a. was the least rewarded of professional men and remained so, although his lot has greatly improved. Yet there has never been a shortage of applicants except at graduate level in mathematics and sciences. Indeed, it can be argued that the adequacy of the supply has been the chief depressant of salaries. Why pay more when intelligent working-class boys and girls are so keen to get away from the workshop and the counter into a safe, pensioned white-collared job? The governments of their day have always been content to control supply and qualifications, retract or expand as the need has arisen, knowing that they will have an adequate supply pool from an aspirant artisan class.

Even now the D.E.S. has been tentatively trying to restrict entry qualifications to O-levels, although in a free academic market the holders of A-levels will have freedom of career choice. Even now, and far too often, we hear the solemn announcements, sometimes from teachers themselves, that it isn't the possession of A-levels or degrees that 'makes a teacher', nor yet B.Ed.s and M.Ed.s and three-year courses—as though there were some mystical and divine afflatus that makes a teacher which is in danger of being deflated by qualifications and training. This kind of thing is right up the street of the civil service, which is responsible for supply and the members of which seem at times to think that the infant schools need to be staffed only by big-breasted motherly girls who are fond of children. Now, however, that we are in danger of a superfluity of teachers, the D.E.S. has cautiously suggested that students opting for primary training should have passed in mathematics and English O-level. Ninety-seven per cent already pass in English anyway.

But the D.E.S. is now facing, and with some uneasiness, a completely new problem in that it may well lose control over teacher-supply. This may suit immediate policy in view of the hoped-for levelling out of supply and demand in the late Seventies —but you never know! Moreover, if students have freer chance of higher education with no professional strings attached, adequate teacher-recruitment cannot be guaranteed unless salaries and conditions of service are made attractive enough, and the status of the profession is enhanced.

A new situation is arising. With the expansion of higher education in the post-Robbins era, the need to sign on the dotted line of teacher commitment is losing its compulsion. After so many years of expanding recruitment and with a national annual intake stabilised at 39,000, the colleges are falling short of their target with a slight but steady decrease in the percentage of candidates possessing A-levels. The number of applicants with A-levels has, in any case, not increased over the last ten years although the total number of sixth-formers obtaining A-levels has almost doubled. Nor is it insignificant that the wastage both of men and of women during the course and in the first three years of teaching has been increasing.

There is no doubt that the colleges of education could expand in the professional and the non-professional fields of higher education and contribute substantially to its expansion. If this means a decline in commitment at eighteen and a corresponding need to make the teaching profession attractive to high-quality entrants, the better it will be for the profession and for the schools.

3 Primary school teachers

David Fletcher

'Primary school teachers make me sick. They are caught between old methods and new, between authoritarian teaching and guided learning. They know the old methods are dead, but they don't have the self-confidence to take up the new ones. They are confused about what they are supposed to be doing but they don't spend time going on courses to try to find out. I haven't much time for my colleagues.'

A forthright young primary teacher talking. Her views are not typical but they underline the changes now taking place in primary schools. The problems engendered by these changes are real to teachers, but largely misunderstood outside the schools. Listen to the public's views of teachers as recorded a couple of years ago in a survey commissioned by the National Union of Teachers. Comments about teachers included: 'It's something anybody can do. The pay is good for the hours they work. They are attracted by the fact that they can find an outlet for their domineering tendencies over children. They are people who enjoy a captive audience—talkers, extroverts. They watch the traffic pass through . . . secluded, a little isolated. Many teachers don't know where they stand—they don't know what industry and production are about.'

There will obviously be as many teachers' views of their job as there are teachers, and different teachers have different problems. Heather Phillips' problem was an appalling training, compounded by lack of help at her first school. But at the age of only 29 she is now deputy head of a Croydon primary school, and has clearly overcome her initial difficulties. She is a likable fair-haired girl with a determined face, and very decided views about her training in a Welsh college. She said of it: 'The first two or three months were spent messing around while the staff sorted out the courses. When these did get going they were like an extension of school. I did history and geography. History consisted of little more than extensive note-taking, instead of the university attitude I had expected of "Here are the books to read, let's discuss them".

'The geography lecturer was a failed grammar school teacher. When she went for a cup of tea in the afternoon she locked students in her room so that they wouldn't skive off. The course itself was just a re-hash of what I had done at A-level. I also did a course in professional maths with an exam at the end of the second year. During the exam, while the lecturer was pre-occupied, the other students quite literally passed my paper round to one another checking their answers. I think I was just unlucky in my training. I can't believe other colleges are nearly as bad.'

She was equally dissatisfied with her periods of teaching practice because she felt she never had time to get to know the children in her class, and build up a relationship with them. She spent all her time doing 'showy projects' and writing up immaculately neat notes for the lecturer. She felt students on teaching practice would learn much more if they were treated as apprentice teachers, having to mix paints, and listen to children reading, for a term or more rather than trying to be 'real' teachers for three weeks.

'The result of it all was that when I took my first job *I was totally unable to teach*. It was a very old-fashioned formal school, streamed, with eight lessons a day. I got the bottom stream of eight-year-olds. They were very thick, and really needed help. They got me, the second probationary teacher in two years. There were two non-readers, and *I did not know how to teach reading*. I got no help from the senior staff and just muddled through, teaching the way I was taught at school—which is what most teachers do unless they make an effort to break away. One quickly adopts the habits of the school, and I found myself giving weekly spelling tests. John James was a quick boy who hardly bothered to look at the list all week. He got 20 out of 20 in the weekly test, a gold star, and stood up to be clapped by the class. Pat Jones was ever so hard-working, spent half an hour a night all week learning the spellings, only to get three right, and be told to stay in at playtime. I knew the methods were wrong, but *I quickly fell into the ways of the school.*

'Discipline was another problem. If a child misbehaved you didn't try to exercise any control, you simply sent him to the head who made him stand in a corridor. Sometimes there were 20 kids standing there. I muddled through that first year. When I left school at 4 p.m. that was it. I didn't worry about the children because I didn't think there was anything I could do about it. In the second year I realised how desperately *unprepared* I was to teach, and set about remedying it. I went to art and craft courses first. I wanted to know how to teach art to seven-year-olds, and later how to make history and geography mean something to C-stream children.'

In effect she started retraining herself in her spare time. At school she started making children *do* things; instead of telling them that there were eight pints in a gallon, she let them find out by measuring how many pints of water it took to fill a gallon container. Having learnt the fairly basic lesson that children learn by doing, not by being told, she found there was a complete lack of 'doing' equipment in the school—cuisenaire rods, dienes blocks, beads, counters and measuring equipment. She also came to realise that it was not always the children's fault if they didn't understand what they were supposed to be learning. There was a temptation to dismiss as stupid the 11-year-old who asked, when given a subtraction sum to do, whether he should take the top line of numbers from the bottom line, or vice versa.

She commented: 'They often did not know what they were doing. It was simply rote learning of what processes to go through when doing a subtraction. There was no understanding of what it meant to subtract one number from another. There were children in the top year of the juniors who didn't know the answer if you asked "What number is one more than ten?" They could count perfectly well up to 20 or 100 but did not understand the value of number.'

In her second year she had the fourth-year C-stream juniors. They were noisy, rude and lacking in concentration. The work they were expected to do was not geared for their needs, but was a watered-down version of what the A-stream were doing. She gradually realised that they were restless, and lacking in concentration, because the work they were being given was unsuitable.

'Halfway through the year I sat down one night, put my head down and cried and cried. I swore I would never go back to school again. I couldn't stand it any more. Of course I did go back and gradually achieved a relationship with the children in the class. After that I started to climb uphill, and develop as a teacher. I went on several courses to remedy the defects of my college training. I started to get to know the children and how to handle them. Many of the kids were from bad home backgrounds, and *I had absolutely no training* in how to handle disciplinary situations.'

After five years she moved to a very progressive school using the integrated day system—which appealed to her enormously. The school was run by a man whose methods she greatly admired. She found children maturing earlier than in her previous school because the emphasis was on self-discipline rather than on children being disciplined. The children were resourceful and learnt to find their own way around books. Whereas in the first school children would come up and say 'I've finished this page, miss, what do I do next?', in the new school they worked things out for themselves, and told the staff what they were doing.

Margaret Roper's problem is different. Like Heather Phillips she has come to the conclusion that the integrated day is by far the best way of teaching primary school children. But the cost in emotional strain on the teacher is so great that she doesn't know how long she will be able to continue teaching in the present situation. She is a dark-haired young married woman teacher of 30 working in a London slum. On the day I spoke to her, her arm was badly cut and bruised, where a hysterical nine-year-old had dug in her fingernails during a classroom tantrum. Like Heather Phillips she has moved from a very formal school to a very free one, but Margaret, unlike Heather, feels she has moved from the frying pan into the fire.

She said: 'I hope I am helping children to cope with whatever happens to them after they leave school. If you are going to have a permissive society you have got to help them cope with the sort of freedoms which they will have and which we never had. I used to love teaching because I felt I was stimulating and exciting children; too often now I feel that I am just calming them down.'

Describing the formal school at which she had previously taught she said: 'The discipline was fairly strict and children were streamed on the basis of marks they gained in an exam taken at the end of each year. The same exam had been set for the past five years, and the head insisted on streaming the children rigidly on the results of these tests. I didn't agree with it but just handed the results in to him. The discipline was strict, but there was a large number of immigrant children, and they seem to respond to a firm control.'

Disliking the rigidity she moved to a totally free school, using the integrated day approach, in a neighbouring area. There were still a high proportion of immigrants, of children with disturbed backgrounds, and of limited attainment, but the school organisation was totally different. The classroom walls had been knocked down and a corridor taken into the now open teaching area. Staffing was generous—there were six teachers for the 160 children using the open area. The school is totally unstreamed and, apart from daily groupings for maths and English, the children are free to spend their time on whatever work they wish. Each teacher gives the children a certain amount of work to do in their own time, and the children can go to that teacher for help during the free activity periods.

Margaret Roper said: 'There are a great number of advantages in this system. The stress that can develop in an enclosed classroom is eased. Children don't have to stay together—they can move into another area when they feel like it. It is easy to put children of a similar ability together for maths or reading. They can be in different groups for different subjects. In this situation children have the freedom they want. It's good for them to organise their own work, and it helps to teach them self-reliance It is also very good for the teacher to have other teachers around. It enables you to see how other teachers go about solving the sort of problems we all have, what will "work" with children, and what other teachers bring to the job. One of the snags with teaching is that in the normal classroom situation you rarely see other teachers at work, and therefore don't learn from your colleagues.'

The problems of the integrated day system mostly stemmed from classroom organisation. There was a lot of untidiness and it was very difficult to keep control of equipment. Margaret Roper carried a bag around with her containing all her equipment like a sort of portable desk. Teachers wasted a lot of time checking that they had got all their equipment. Activity time was often marred by a group of children wandering about not wanting to do anything constructive. Some teachers had a habit of sitting in a corner with a group of children and ignoring what went on around them.

She said: 'Working all day in this kind of situation asks an awful lot of the teacher. It's emotionally and physically exhausting Idealistically I am sure this system is right. There is so much that is good, and for every child that is rude, or appallingly aggressive, there are another six who are happy and creative. But the free methods, combined with the rough kids in this particular area, make it terribly tiring for the staff. If only you can stick it for long enough, if you are dedicated enough, you may win through. Many of the teachers just put in their notice.

'Discipline is a constant problem. I call myself working class, but I did not have the rough disturbed background of some of my children. I think it is essential that there should be more teachers who can talk to a child with a disturbed background from an emotionally sympathetic standpoint. The situation in school is eased so much if there are teachers who are familiar with these children's backgrounds and therefore with their problems. Time spent in an adventure playground, or perhaps working with a probation officer, would help. These sorts of thing should qualify for extra grants.

'I think the attitude of children has changed in the ten years I have been teaching; it reflects a change in attitude at home. It is less often assumed now that the school knows best. The general questioning of authority which now takes place in society at large has caused a new atmosphere to prevail in the classroom. It's not that children are naughty, it is just that you have to fight to be heard in the first place. What do you do when children misbehave? You don't hit them, you don't send them to the head any more. My automatic reaction to a child being naughty is to explain why its action was wrong. I sometimes think I am not tough enough, that I am too emotionally involved with the children.'

Some of the problems would at least be eased if it were not for the general poverty of provision. The area consists of Victorian terraced houses, and old houses split into multi-occupation. The school is old, and one of the work areas is so inadequately heated that it can't be used in winter. The school is bursting at the seams with children. One partitioned-off corner, used as a quiet room, had to be given up to the infant school when infant numbers expanded unexpectedly, and there was nowhere else to house them. Teachers sell biscuits at playtime, and use the slender profits to buy coloured pencils. Proper woodwork facilities are lacking ('a few hammers and nails would get rid of an awful lot of ill-feeling among children').

Margaret Roper was trained to teach junior children, and she says it was generally assumed that juniors would be just about able to read. *In fact she found a lot of juniors could not read.** 'I had to rack my brains for ways of organising them so that they could learn. I did not find so much difficulty in the actual teaching of reading, it was the organisation of the class so that other groups of children are usefully occupied while you go round to each group in turn for reading. It was class organisation that I was taught very little about at college and had to pick up for myself as I went along. I don't remember any mention of i.t.a. when I was at college; most of the books listed as suitable reading material were the very conventional children's books such as *Black Beauty*.† Books

* Cf. comments in chapters by Nicholas Bagnall and Frances Verrinder—Editor.
† Cf. comments in Ronald Deadman's chapter on Miss Austen—Editor.

have improved so fantastically in the last 10 years. Equipment is so marvellous now if only we could afford to have it in the class-rooms.'

While Margaret Roper wonders whether she has the stamina to keep up the struggle for her deprived children, Hilary Pannell's classroom situation is the envy of many teachers although some might feel it a soft option. She has one young son, and has been teaching for four years, the last two of them at a pleasant light airy junior school at Blackheath, South London. The children are very articulate, immigrants are rare. The children are frequently taken out to restaurants by their parents, and ask her the next morning whether she too likes asparagus tips cooked in butter. Parents invite her to their homes for dinner, and send her receipes for pizza pie.

She said: 'The children nearly all come from homes where conversation is a normal part of home life. There are some work-ing-class children, but they are all articulate. They are used to discussing, and we cover a lot of topics in school—whether they believe in God, whether girls are better than boys, whether TV is good or bad. At this school you can get on with the teaching and do not have to think all the time about social training.' She has not always worked with such stimulating children. After getting what she considers an exceptionally good training at the very progressive Goldsmiths' College, she taught in a run-of-the-mill primary school where the children were of average ability and the school was run in a fairly formal way.

'I started there full of enthusiasm for teaching by projects and remember doing a very exciting project about the sea. It covered wrecks, crabs, explorers, and we did graphs of animals in the sea. It was very successful but none of the staff at school seemed to understand what I was doing. The head paid lip service to modern methods, but I don't think she really believed in them. To her I was just a good art teacher and the only response I got to my project teaching was "Can you knock up a few dollies, dear?" She was happy if she came in and saw all the children at their desks working hard. She never stopped me using my methods, but just thought I was cranky. At least the inspector knew what I was doing, and that gave me some encouragement. I left the school convinced that project teaching was the right method. The children were so enthusiastic, but they were not articulate. I found it difficult to get discussions going with them. They responded best to short barking phrases, but that was not my way.'

Her experience of the two schools has led her to believe that it is wrong to 'stream' children. Nor does she believe in the wide-spread primary practice of having one table for bright children, one or two for the in-betweens and one for the dull children. She said: 'Children in my class sit wherever they want. Some of the closest friendships between children cut right across class barriers. I could never stream children after seeing how well non-streaming works.'

'My bright children do not suffer and I have seen so many examples of children benefiting. There was one very shy little girl whose brothers and sisters were very thick. She was very quiet in the infants' school and had a lot of time off. She was good at art, and it gradually dawned on me that she was quite bright. She was accepted by the other children and benefited enormously from her contact with them. Had she been in a streamed school I think that even the most well-meaning head might have put her in a lower stream and moved her from the very children who would have helped her. Non-streaming also benefits the bright children. They are sometimes very impressed by the drawings of a child who is not as quick as they are at other subjects. I can remember the envy children felt for one boy who was very slow learning to write, but who could do marvellous artistic work.'

The situation in Joan Green's school is just the opposite. Instead of having a classroom full of bright, inquiring minds of children from a trendy and fashionable area, with lots of open spaces and trees, she has a class of deprived children in a 90-year-old school from one of Birmingham's twilight areas. She came to Birmingham almost by chance from her native Yorkshire after completing her training 12 years ago. She has continued to teach deprived children by choice ever since, because of the satisfaction she gets from feeling she is doing something to compensate for their backgrounds.

She said: 'I did my final teaching practice in Harrogate, and when I came to Birmingham *I had no idea of how the difficulties of poor housing and a bad social environment could affect children's learning in school.** There is no background of education in the home and a dearth of books. The children are presented with a world of books and literature and imagination at school, but when they go home it is completely blank, there is just the TV. Overcrowding at home also often means that children do not get sufficient rest at night and come to school tired.'

For 10 years she taught in an area which was gradually filling with immigrants, as resourceful parents moved out to Birmingham's greener suburbs. There were no immigrants when she started at the school; 10 years later 30 per cent of the pupils were immigrants, many of them from the West Indies with very different assumptions and backgrounds. Coupled with this difficulty of their different cultural heritage they found themselves living in slum conditions alongside indigenous children who were deprived.

'I grew up with the problem, and learned as I went along, but it is a very difficult situation into which to put new teachers. Many of them have trained in rural areas, but they will spend most of their lives teaching in urban areas, where the school problems are quite different. They are completely unprepared for the bounce, vivacity and irrepressibility of West Indian children. They may fail to realise that these children have a language problem; it is assumed they speak English, but in fact it is a very strange variety of English. I had a child last week who came to school for the first time, and was very aggressive, because he could not make himself understood to the other children.

'It is very important to understand their background. Children in a great many West Indian schools are taught in the old monitorial system. They are all crammed into desks and no one is allowed to move. Put a child who has been used to this sort of classroom situation into an informal classroom, and it is no wonder he does not know how to adapt. It helps immigrants quite a lot if you can be a little formal until they see how to fit into the new

* Cf. comments in Dr Midwinter's chapter—Editor.

classroom situation. I would be happier if student teachers spent more time in school, doing more practical classroom work, with more co-operation between practising teachers and the colleges, and with fewer academics supervising teachers. You still find examples of lecturers trying to teach students for age ranges of which they have no experience.'

With the exception of Hilary Pannell, who thought a great deal of the training given at Goldsmiths', the other three teachers all felt their training had been inadequate in some respects. In particular they criticised the way they had been taught to teach maths and reading. None felt totally 'at home' with maths. Classroom organisation and discipline were also topics which they felt were skimped in training. All had felt the need to go on in-service training courses within a short time of starting teaching to remedy the deficiencies of their training. The unfortunate thing is that there are thousands of teachers who muddle through without bothering to make up the shortcomings of their training.

4 Secondary school teachers

Frances Verrinder

Teachers in secondary schools are confused about their rôle in society and the nature of their jobs. They are often extremely critical about factors affecting their income and profession.

I talked to some secondary school staff in an effort to discover the causes of their discontent. I wanted to give them an opportunity to speak from the classroom to those who determine their salaries and status. The teachers came from all kinds of schools: an approved school, secondary modern schools, comprehensives, grammar schools, two public schools (both day—one girls-only, one boys-only), and a private boarding school. They were in the three age groups, 21 to 27, 28 to 40, and the over-40s. The sample were equally divided between men and women. It was interesting that the majority of the women had no conception of teaching as a 'career' in the sense that this word is normally used. The unmarried women who were not engaged expected to get married, have children, and then return to what they regarded a 'useful job' when their own children reached school age. This view of the job was, of course, shared by those women in middle age and over-40 groups who had done just this. The great majority of the 21 to 27, and the 28 to 40 age groups were graduates who had usually taken a one-year postgraduate diploma of education. Just under half the 40-plus age group had a two-year certificate of education from a college of education.

I questioned them about pay, conditions of work, the curriculum, relations with colleagues and with the head, the status of the profession, and their overall satisfaction with their lot. Not

surprisingly they considered they were not paid enough. Predict-
ably women teachers tended to be less worried about pay than
men. One girl of 23 with an upper second-class degree, and
a postgraduate certificate of education, teaching biology at a
progressive private boarding school, was earning £1,400, and
was almost apologetic about it. It was as though she suspected
something was wrong about such a salary for someone of her age
and qualifications. But she could not be sure whether it was too
little or too much! 'I mean it's *quite* good–especially for a girl of
my age, isn't it?' she asked. One part-time married woman
returner, who taught physics at a girls' grammar school, was much
more down-to-earth about money. She saw her salary purely as
a supplement to her husband's, a source of extra luxuries for her
family.

But, in general, both men and women who regarded teaching
as a profession in which they intended to make a career were both
angry and ambivalent about pay. They were angry because
they felt it was too low—and ambivalent because many
suspected perhaps some of their colleagues were not worth more.
There was no evidence of doubts about their own ability to give
the education service value for money. Younger teachers felt that
they were badly paid because the public had insufficient respect
for their profession. They also pointed out that this lack of status
was reinforced by the low salaries. A 27-year-old head-of-
department at a day public school said: 'Most people think anyone
can stand in front of a class, and talk, and that it does not require
any real or specialised skills. The trouble is that a good teacher—
who's communicating his stuff—makes it look too easy.'

Some of the men in their 30s were really quite badly off. One
deputy head of department, earning £2,200, thought it was
difficult to keep a wife, three children, and pay a large mortgage.
'It sounds a lot—I know,' he said, 'but if my wife didn't work as
well we'd be very hard up.' It was generally believed by the men
that salaries had been artificially held down since the 1930s—when
according to popular myth teachers were well paid—by the
preponderance of women in the profession. Women were often
thought to regard the profession as a social service, a vocation,

and to believe that it was 'not right' to demand the appropriate financial rewards.

I asked the 27-year-old head of the department how he assessed the value of his job. He said: 'I suppose I sometimes feel as though my work is amazingly easy compared with, say, an engineer's or a systems analyst's. Indeed, my conditions of work are easy. My firm is not going to go bankrupt or make me redundant! It's very unlikely I'll ever get the sack. This security is worth a good deal. But I think the responsibilities and the level of my skills are just as great as those of an engineer or systems analyst. I teach A-level sociology and economics, and if you paid me on results I'd do quite well. I think I'm worth about £3,500, but I suspect that this is only because I can't see myself *ever* earning so much.'

The teachers were in general agreement about pay and holidays. Holidays were seen as necessary periods of recuperation. One newly graduated art teacher said that she only began to feel human again at the end of the second week of any holiday. She was obviously finding her work emotionally exhausting, possibly the result of her lack of experience. Yet even older teachers in their 30s admitted to exhaustion at the end of term. Long holidays, and to a lesser extent the short working day, were seen not as perks but as *essential aids to sanity*. All the teachers claimed to prepare most of their lessons, and to spend most evennings, and part of their week-ends, marking papers. Apart from these two factors their attitudes and lives varied enormously. A look at four teachers, working in different kinds of school, illustrates the diversity of secondary school jobs. It also reveals how each job needs a completely individual approach. It raises the problem of whether the present system of training can *adequately prepare teachers for the variety of 'rôles' in secondary schools.*

*　　　*　　　*

Anne, aged 25, upper second-class degree in English at a red-brick university, postgraduate certificate of education, engaged to an Oxford postgraduate; working in an all-girls' inner-ring slum school in Birmingham.

The school buildings are red-brick, 1890s School Board, surrounded by acres of brick rubble, very tatty because the school is always being scheduled for demolition within the next five years, so it never seems worthwhile repainting them. The school is described by Anne as 'laughably comprehensive'—she says all the bright children are creamed off by the city's grammar schools. 'It's really a secondary modern school, although a few pupils do take O-level, and slightly more take C.S.E. I came here to teach O-level English.' She objects to the way the school is run; she thinks the objectives to which it is geared are quite irrelevant to the pupils' lives both now and in the future. 'The head has secret hankerings after a grammar school, I think. She must have because she tries to run this school like one. Even a seventh-rate grammar school would satisfy her. I know she's old and trained 40 years ago, and doesn't see why she should abandon what she would call "her standards", and what I would call her irrelevant and unrealistic attitudes. What is the point of trying to make the Pakistani and Indian girls wear school uniform, and of forbidding their saris and Shalwari?

'The school has about 800 pupils, of whom 90 per cent are Indians, Pakistanis, West Indians and Irish. Many of the children suffer from the disadvantages common in slum-clearance areas like this: one-parent families, large numbers of brothers and sisters, no privacy, no bathrooms, no amenities, and nowhere to play. A high proportion of girls in the "C" and "D" streams are on probation, in the care of the local child-care department, or have come to the notice of the social services in some way.'

She found two years ago, when she began teaching at the school, her diploma of education was 'quite helpful' in dealing with her O-level English language, and her C.S.E. classes. But she also had to teach 'general English—whatever that is' to the third-year 'C' stream, and found *her teacher training quite inappropriate*. 'The third-year "C" stream are the failures, the duds. They know it. They are going to make sure you know it by being hell to teach. I was supposed to read *Pride and Prejudice* with them, which I consider a sort of macabre joke.' (Note here the unsuitable material and compare the comments in Ronald Deadman's chapter

'The Teaching of Reading' where he says: 'If they provided a reading list which included Wesker, Sillitoe . . . and excluded Miss Austen'—Editor.)' 'Instead I got them to write about themselves, and realised when I saw the results that *I really need primary school skills*, how to teach reading and writing. They all wrote with great difficulty, couldn't spell, couldn't express themselves, some could barely read, and they could not concentrate for long.'

It is useful to compare these remarks of Anne, and comments elsewhere in this book, with the words of Dr Joyce Morris in the Introduction to Donald Moyle's book, *The Teaching of Reading*. She wrote: 'There is some evidence that the reading standards of the school population have improved steadily since the Second World War. Nevertheless, the progress made gives no grounds for complacency, since it is estimated that about 10 per cent of school-leavers cannot read well enough to cope with the ordinary day-to-day demands of life in our traditionally literate society. Recent research also indicates that at the other end of the scale of reading potentiality, a sizable proportion of undergraduates have not sufficiently mastered the more complex reading skills to enable them to complete a degree course. Reading disability of one kind or another is therefore a matter for concern in Britain.'

Anne was alarmed by her pupils' inability to grasp the point of simple news items on TV. She said: 'They all watched about 30 hours of TV a week *without apparently taking in anything at all*. Nobody could tell me the meaning of the fall of Biafra. The programmes had been full of it all week. They all read comic-strip love-story magazines like the *Valentine*, *Romeo*, as well as *Woman* and *Woman's Own*, and their ideas about love and marriage were largely absorbed from these.'

She also found the school unprepared and seemingly unwilling to cater for the real needs of the children. She said: 'There was, and is, no arrangement in the school for teaching new immigrant arrivals English in small groups, and there is not enough staff for me to hive off my half-dozen illiterates for special teaching. After a long discussion with the head of the English department about what I was supposed to do with these kids (apart from preventing a riot) I decided to try an unconventional approach.

'I reckoned it was useless to try and teach them to read, write, and comprehend in the usual formalised way. Instead we read things they liked, starting off with *Valentine*, and discussing the stories; then we looked at some Elizabethan love poems which started off two main projects—what it was like to live in those days, and discussions on love and marriage. The TV series on the wives of Henry VIII provided the focus for an enormous amount of discussion on both topics. After Henry VIII we studied Elizabeth, read more love poems, a bit of *Romeo and Juliet*, and then, after an inter-racial fight in the playground, and because one of my class was a member of a Black Power group, we studied the slave trade. We went to the ballet (a miracle of organisation) and soon the classroom was covered with pictures of dancers in improbable leaps. The love and marriage themes went on continuously. The biology department arranged for films on menstruation, and on how babies are born. Even the domestic science teacher told me the girls were much more amenable these days in her cookery lessons.

'I must say that after the first few nerve-racking weeks with 3C, I began to enjoy myself. I came to the conclusion that my academic background and the content of the diploma course were a drawback in teaching non-academic children of this type. The diploma course presupposes everyone is going to teach academic subjects to bright academic children from clean, airy, middle-class suburbs. I think the only answer is either to rearrange the diploma year so that you have practice in more than one kind of school or to make in-service training immediately and readily available if the young teacher is confronted with a completely different kind of child and ability range. A week of in-service training at the beginning of that September term with 3C would have eliminated many of my trials and errors.

'I was not prepared for the fact that such children often had no sense whatever of *time* for example. They had no conception of the length of 400 years, nor could they place a period in its historical perspective. They seemed aware that "about 100 years ago there was Queen Victoria", and it was generally reckoned that Henry VIII was "a bit before that". My experiences with 3C made me feel extremely inadequate and very angry. Some were horrible to me. They all came from such awful deprived backgrounds. I feel at times I'm more of a social worker than a teacher. I used to rage against the headmistress as she stood in Assembly quoting St Paul on love to those poor kids. Whatever you do it is never enough. Four general English lessons a week cannot begin to undo 15 years of brutalising and hardship.'

*   *   *

Paul, aged 27, a degree in philosophy, politics and economics. An Oxford man. A postgraduate teaching diploma. Head of department in economics at a London day public school for boys. Taught at the school for four years. He became head of department after two years. He is about to leave to work for the B.B.C.

He said: 'I teach A-level pupils mostly, which is jolly satisfying. Not so much because they pass their exams and go on to university (though that *is* satisfying, of course) but because they are intelligent, lively, eager to learn and they present no discipline problems.' He was educated at a private boarding school, and did his teaching practice at Repton, where he had the undeserved reputation for being 'a bit of a Leftie'.

He added: 'I found the Dip.Ed. course absolutely appalling. Subjects like the philosophy of education and curriculum and method were treated so superficially—they were quite useless. I had one visit from my supervisor on teaching practice; in fact I learned far more from the man who was detailed to look after me at Repton. There seemed to be no instruction on the actual practicalities of teaching, how best to stand in front of the class and talk, for example. I gather that at universities like York they have TV now so that you can see yourself doing it, and the other students can comment.' On his reasons for leaving he was refreshingly honest and perceptive—even if he was depressing. He said: 'I like teaching very much but I feel I cannot get any further in it. I'm rather young for a headship, which isn't necessarily teaching anyway, is it? More like management, I should think. I've been very happy—the staff here are very able and friendly. But I think it's time I did something else. If I weren't leaving teaching I would soon become stale, and the quality of my work would fall off. I suspect when a lot of teachers get to about 35 they are really stale. *That's the point at which some of them go and get a job in departments of education.* Perhaps that's why education courses are so bad? In-service training should not be regarded as some sort of perk, but as an integral part of the job, every two or three years. If I were going to be a headmaster, for example, it would be essential for me to be given a valid course on how to run a school. At the moment it is all so *ad hoc* and amateur. Courses like that must be the exception and not the rule. I think the present attitude to training—giving students one or even two years' training and then packing them off into the schools for life—is *criminal.*'

*   *   *

Freda, aged 40, teaches in a school for E.S.N. and maladjusted children in the north-west of England; did a two-year teachers' training certificate in the late 1940s. She began teaching juniors in a slum school near her home in Manchester. After her children were old enough to attend school she returned to teaching, after taking a one-year diploma at the nearest university, and started in a special school.

She said: 'Remedial work is extremely demanding emotionally. It's difficult not to get too involved with the children. We take them up to 16, and the school is run very much like an ordinary primary school. I have one class all the time, except for subjects like physical education and housecraft. My class has nine children at the moment, six boys and three girls ranging from 13 to 16 in age.

'We start off in the morning with a school assembly, prayers and a splendidly out-of-tune hymn. After this I do "number", as it is known in teacher-training courses. I always try to relate what we are learning with everyday things. My kids, if they get jobs, are probably always going to have unskilled monotonous jobs, but they still have to know basic things that the rest of us take for granted, shopping, how to tell the time, look up people in the telephone directory, how to read time-tables, for example. So I base number on real life things. Looking up someone in the phone book, for example, requires a number of different skills— how to spell the person's name, knowledge of the alphabet, writing down the name and phone number as well as actually phoning.

'We do a lot of painting and we have made some puppets; we dance, and swimming is a great favourite. All these things are good for physical co-ordination which can be a source of confidence, and confidence is what the children need, and badly. We are also doing a play about Boadicea and the Romans, although I think that the girls would have preferred Queen Elizabeth I as they have seen her on the telly. The boys, however, wanted to be Romans and ancient Britons, and since they are in a majority, Romans it had to be. So at the moment, we're busy constructing Roman helmets out of papier mâché, and wigs for the ancient Britons out of old nylons. We'll invite parents to the play at the end of term, as we always do. It makes them feel more involved with the school. I am extremely happy in my job; I have a feeling of solid worthwhile achievement which I didn't have even when I taught very bright seven-year-olds. Staff morale is extremely good, and the turnover is very low; I've been here for five years, and there are six of us of whom only one has left to have a baby. The head is approachable, does a good deal of teaching himself and is solidly behind one's attempts to help the children.'

This woman teacher was one of the happier, and more satisfied, I spoke to. Part of the reason for this was, as she said, that 'she'd been specially trained to teach E.S.N. children, and had chosen to do it'. She thought it was the young, and the idealistic, who were most concerned about the teacher's rôle, and function, both in the schools, and in society at large. She said: 'I'm not at all surprised that young teachers are confused about what they're supposed to be doing. In fact I'm surprised they're not more militant really. Most of them come from middle-class grammar schools, and their college of education, or university department, doesn't really disabuse them of the notion that their teaching careers will of course take place in middle-class grammar schools, or purpose-built, uncreamed comprehensives.'

She added: 'Teachers who have a clear objective, getting O- and A-level results, or, like me, coping with the system's rejects, are less likely to worry about their function. It's people in the middle, who are teaching the non-academic streams in comprehensives, or the lower streams in secondary moderns, who must wonder what precisely their rôle is. I used to worry about it before I decided on this—what was I? Entertainer till the school-leaving age released them? Social worker? Moral tutor? Provider of information? It was never at all clear.'

*   *   *

Carol, aged 31, an art specialist; teaches in small girls' grammar school in West Country; husband teaches art in boys' grammar school in the town, both paint, sculpt and make pottery.

She said: 'I am very lucky in the way of facilities. Because the school is used for evening classes, I have several potters' wheels, and a kiln, so I do quite a lot of pottery with the upper school. The whole school up till the fourth year has compulsory art for a double period a week and in a way I like these classes best. It's very satisfying to get the children to express themselves; so many of them are frightened of doing so, and produce stilted little illustrative pictures. Before we came here we lived just outside London, and I used to teach part-time in an approved school for boys near our home. Once they realised they could paint what they liked, I got some lurid, and quite violent, paintings, much more expressive than the timid 13-year-olds in my school now. When I first started to teach I worried about the value of my lessons in particular and of teaching art in general; I got very depressed about it because I was teaching in a big London comprehensive and I felt that art was hardly relevant to the lives of the deprived kids I had to cope with. It was my husband who pointed out that getting 12-year-olds to express themselves in paint was one step towards self-realisation; getting them to appreciate form and colour is another. I know it's true, but I still think it's not enough.'

*   *   *

But perhaps the most alarming person was a forthright, middle-
aged English teacher in a Tyneside comprehensive school who
glared at me when I asked him if I could interview him about his
work: 'If you really care about the kids, education and all, why
aren't you bloody teaching yourself?'

Part 2

The case against teachers and training

5 The rejects

Keith Gardner

'What did you think of school?'

Jim looked at the ground, scuffed a stone across the pavement, shrugged, and muttered, 'I don't know.'

I had asked the wrong question. In Jim's mind I was already classified as 'one of Them'. The barriers were up. A friendly conversation about cars, girls and modern gear had come to an end. The single word 'school' had been sufficient to alarm and cause the mental defences to muster. Significantly, Jim had used the familiar smoke-screen of the classroom . . . 'I don't know.'

Jim is 17. He left school at 14.

That is a statement of fact. He missed a year of compulsory education by simply not turning up. Apparently, neither headmaster nor Local Education Authority were too energetic in attempting to enforce the law. They accepted the inevitable. Jim was exercising his initiative in a way that gave his teachers cause for relief.

What is Jim like today? He can read a little, write a little, and add up the money in his pocket. He can thieve a little, fight a little, and can make a pound or two when the spirit moves him. Legality and illegality, right and wrong, are concepts that scarcely trouble him. Opportunity, need or necessity seem to be the immediate determinants of his actions. He is top priority for a visit from the police when anything happens within five miles of his house. They caught him out . . . once. The experience did him good. But the police reckon he will be a little too clever one day, then they will get him.

Incidentally, Jim was labelled 'dull' by his school. I am left to ponder the nature of a dullness that enables a youth to steer an uncertain course with a native cunning that effectively wards off all attempts to socialise or reform. He has drifted through seven or eight jobs. One, at least, was respectable and held some prospect of a future. It lasted a few weeks. Jim could not take orders. 'Too bloody bossy,' was Jim's own summary of the craftsman who took him on.

It took a long time to piece together the fragments of that particular episode. I had to sift the comments from the family. Jim, himself, had nothing to say. It seems, however, that a well-intentioned man took it upon himself to put Jim right with the minimum delay. The result was a running battle and Jim walked out.

Another job held no prospects but paid reasonable money. At the end of the third week a pay packet went missing. It was predictable that the first suspect was Jim. He had a reputation. In this case he was probably innocent, but the accusation was enough to provide an excuse for not turning up again.

Jim's father was quick to point out that his son had never been sacked. This may or may not be true. The point is that family pride and family loyalty demanded some grain of respect for Jim. 'He's never been sacked.' There was a ring of pride in the statement—an implicit recognition that Jim was clever enough to anticipate the event. And cleverness in the face of authority was a quality that Jim's father admired. Jim himself has his own superficial reasons for never sticking at a job. They are quite plausible. Behind the catalogue of bad working conditions, unsympathetic mates, being the centre of practical jokes, however, there were deeper issues. One emerged with startling clarity when, in a sudden rush of confidence, Jim asked me, 'Would you stick being kicked around?'

It's a fair question. The honest answer is 'No'. But if Jim and I share this sentiment that is where the comparison ends. I, at least, am able to do my own share of kicking in what I hope is a reasonable way. When Jim kicks back he merely increases his chances of being fouled again.

A psychiatrist would probably have a theory about all this.

A social worker produced a trite label—'Of course, Jim has a personality defect. He needs treatment.' As a layman I can only reflect that Jim has already had 'treatment' of a kind. His own recollections of part of this treatment were relayed to me by his sister. Jim would rarely talk about school.

When he was about six he complained, 'They don't like my dad. They blame me for everything.' That was the infant school. Serious truanting began in the junior school. A running battle with the 'School Man' began. When prosecution was threatened, Dad attempted persuasion with Jim in the shape of a beating. Jim went back to school, and was met with a caning. He went on truanting.

His activities are recounted in a series of jerky sentences, each one prised out of him by my questions.

'What did you do when you played hookey?'

'Nothing.'

'You must have done something.'

'. . . went in the shops.'

Going into shops involved both legal and illegal operations. If Jim had succeeded in begging, earning or stealing an odd coin or two, he could buy. Sweets and cigarettes were the most desired goods. Woolworths was the main target on penniless days. There the sweets were laid out on open counters and, unlike the supermarkets, there was no cash desk near the door. Cigarettes were smoked in favourite hiding places, company was gained by haunting the building sites or the market. The market had to be treated carefully. Whilst there was always an odd copper to be made, helping out, there was also danger from the 'School Man' who occasionally prowled around looking for absentees.

Jim remembered one day his school had a special holiday. He went to the market and helped on a stall. Along came the 'School Man'. Jim's story fell on deaf ears. He was hauled back to the empty school. His sense of outrage at this miscarriage of justice is still evident eight years later. Secondary school is remembered with more clarity and detail. 'Teachers!' Jim mouths the word and enunciates a venom into two short syllables that is best left to the imagination.

Sarcasm, impatience, despotism, teasing and bullying were the main weapons of his sworn enemy; each single incident, in itself of little moment, trivial, even understandable, yet cumulatively there was a barrage of horrifying intensity. School became a treadmill of senseless time-wasting in which only the hopeless fight against authority had meaning. Jim summarised some of the points of conflict. 'Me hair . . . me trousers . . . and me smell.' The comments on the school reports run true to form. 'Lazy . . . No interest . . . Needs firm discipline . . . No ability whatsoever. . . .' Now let Jim comment on the comments. 'What do they know?' 'Who do they think they are?'

What has Jim gained from his long years of intermittent schooling?

He is barely literate, has very little general knowledge of an approved variety, is ignorant of the binary system. Religious education, history, science, English, music, and games seem to have passed him by. Yet every self-destroying notion and idea seems to have established itself beyond the point of remedy. What he has learned he has learned well. Of course, there are individuals who were interested in Jim. I met his remedial teacher. He remembered Jim. 'Yes . . . a queer lad. I was the only one who understood him. Might have got somewhere with him if he hadn't stayed off so much. But . . .'

Jim remembered his remedial teacher. 'Silly bugger. Tried to butter me up.'

The local detective will stop on the street and talk to Jim. Perhaps he has his eye on future crime figures when he trundles out his well-meaning advice. 'What you need is five years in the Army. They'll lick you into shape.'

A friend once succeeded in getting Jim through the doors of a College of Further Education. All seemed well until it came to the inevitable forms. 'Just fill this in.' Jim reacted violently to the unreadable questions and that was the end of that.

It is tempting to pause at this point and condemn the school system, the uncomprehending teachers, the rejection of the non-academic pupil. However, I must ask myself, 'Would I have been a better teacher in the same situation?' I doubt it. Looking back, I realise that I was completely unprepared to deal with the Jims of this world. Perhaps in the battle for survival in the classroom I have played my part in moulding the rejects, albeit innocently and without premeditation. I just didn't know what I was doing.

In any case, the non-academic pupil does not always turn out like Jim. His sister is a case in point. Sandra is more articulate than Jim. She is making frantic efforts to escape from her working-class label. Yet there is a sense in which she presents an even more disturbing picture. To her, school is equated with being pushed to one side. She remembers references to her family when she was in the infant school. 'They're a bad lot.' Her reaction was to retire out of sight to avoid being noticed, then in the misery of isolation she would seek sudden recognition. She chose her moments badly and was often repulsed.

Then she discovered that she was articulate. 'I used to talk and talk,' she said, 'just to make friends. I made up stories. So the teacher told the class I was a liar.' In the junior school she was placed in the lowest class. 'We were ignored,' she said. 'We knew they only had time for the 11-plus classes.'

Eventually, Sandra sat the selection examination herself. She claims she never knew it was the 11-plus test. To quote her words: 'The teacher said we were having another test. We had to do our best and not worry.' She had done practice tests before. This time, she decided the questions were stupid, so she just drew patterns on the paper.

Sandra went to the secondary modern school. There she was determined to show 'Them' what she could do. She worked hard and gained some useful grades in her C.S.E. examination.

But what did she think about school?

Unlike Jim, Sandra will talk about her teachers. Whether it is fact or fiction it is a record of what she believes. She chooses her words carefully when she speaks. Often I got the impression she was trying to unravel a mystery. To her, teachers are a race apart; they say things about people that are not true; they think they are always right; they don't understand that working-class children are as frightened of poetry as the art mistress is of quadratic equations; they make impossible demands; they expect everyone to be perfect at everything; they have one law for themselves and another for kids; they are often cruel—perhaps without knowing it. Indeed, the cruelty of school seems to dominate her mind. She wasn't referring to the cruelty of cuff and cane, but to the insidious effects of not meeting expectations and of being made to feel inadequate and inferior.

Once, over a cup of coffee, Sandra gave me a blinding glimpse of her own thinking. We were talking about school. Suddenly, she blurted out: 'My dad has called me worse than muck. That doesn't matter. He doesn't know anything. But teachers . . . they make you believe they are something. They kid you they're almighty. Then they knock you down. That matters. So you stop thinking teachers are almighty.'

In that moment I saw the toughs that I had taught. The ones who could take anything. The ones I thought were schooled to feel little and care less. And I wondered. . . .

Today Sandra is working part-time on two A-level subjects. She has made good. Yet she believes that it is in spite of, not because of, school. She may have refuted her junior school label—'Lacks ability and concentration—' but she still smarts under the final epithet on the day she left school—'You've done very well considering what a bad start you had.' It was the last reminder that she was not really accepted.

These children come from the same home, but they are quite different people. Yet they share a common belief. They regret going to school and they distrust teachers. It is one thing to collect statistics, interview samples, prepare questionaires, and produce a report. It is quite another matter to get to know two youngsters quite well and be faced with the realities of being born 'working class'. Perhaps the subject is more suitable for a play or a novel than an educational article. A sample of two is insignificant; their views and statements are unreliable; their recollections are biased. All this is true. Equally, for the first time in my life I begin to understand what it means to be a non-academic pupil. I am beginning to know Jim and Sandra as real people. I believe that real people, not statistics and classifications, are the subject-matter of education.

If this is accepted, then I can make certain deductions. Firstly, it is clear that Jim and Sandra were forced into a system that could not accept them. At best, they were tolerated or endured. It is not my purpose to allot blame. They must have been difficult pupils to handle. At times, however, one is forced to conclude that some teachers are remarkably insensitive.

Secondly, it seems to me that, for Jim and Sandra, school often meant a meaningless passage of time more productive of frustration than positive learning. They knew they were misfits. They failed to adapt; school failed in its efforts to change them.

Thirdly, I am convinced that whilst I could isolate a mass of theoretical issues from the story of Jim and Sandra, what needs to be looked at most closely is the question of human relationships within school. There are other problems, but it is in the day-to-day rough and tumble of teacher and pupil that the seeds of enduring attitudes are sown.

Fourthly, I am aware that I may have selected two special cases. Note how I drop into the professional jargon! These youngsters are real people, not cases. Perhaps they are exceptional, but as I drive through the sombre streets of the old city where I work, or venture into the gaunt housing estates, I have the evidence of my eyes. I fear they are part of a majority, not a minority. They are exceptional only because they have expressed a common human need in their own exceptional way.

Surely, therefore, I am entitled to ask: 'Must teachers always be trained as if their task is to carry on the tradition of catering for the academic minority?' Is there an alternative? We can attempt to find one.

For instance, we might begin by considering who goes to school rather than who is fit to teach. It must be wrong to start with assumptions about what minimal academic qualifications are essential for teacher training, or what subject specialisms should be provided, or what professional knowledge is respectable, and ignore the raw material upon which teachers will exercise their craft.

Jim and Sandra are but two examples of a mass of children who enter school far removed from the world of those who people the academic greenhouse that nurtures the A-level, college, and postgraduate courses. Teachers are selected because they are different. Jim and Sandra found this out in their own painful way.

Perhaps differences could be overcome if we concentrated more on selecting people who could communicate with children. But communication is not just a matter of finding a common language or a common interest. To communicate with Jim and Sandra one must make them feel accepted and be acceptable to them.

Progressive infant education is achieving a great deal in breaking down the barriers between teacher and pupil in a realistic way. But the demands on the teacher are immense. At the present time 'progressive' methods appear to be suitable only for those teachers who have a happy knack of handling children in an informal way. The challenge is to find a way of helping more people to acquire the knack.

One must also inquire into a content of education that is realistic for the majority. This is provocative territory. Positions are already polarised. If a progressive move is made today a letter will appear in a respectable newspaper tomorrow deploring the lowering of academic standards. If human happiness is viewed as a proliferation of labour-saving devices, hygienic packaging, and expendable luxuries, then we must produce scientists, engineers, mathematicians, programmers, accountants and managers to feed the technological monster. If we are determined to press headlong into an ecological disaster, then we had better carry on just as we are. If we are determined to continue a division of men into those who can and those who can't, then we had better leave things just as they are. If, however, we are really concerned about creating a world that is worth living in, then we need a deeper concern for people.

This is not to deny an academic tradition. It is merely a plea for the application of humanity to a difficult situation. Producing a weak facsimile of the academic tradition in our schools is not enough. The application of academic integrity to developing personal growth through education is a much more viable objective.

Thus, the question facing us is not whether we should train teachers to sustain a traditional academic tradition, but whether our academic tradition has given us the breadth of vision to design a pattern for meaningful mass education. It is not the first time that academic tradition has been challenged. If it were, I might be writing this chapter in Latin.

Now I come to the question: 'If I had to go back over the years and had to train to be a teacher again, what would I ask for that would fit me to work with Jim and Sandra?'

I am sure of one thing. One element in my education should have been more contact with students studying in different fields. It is the isolation of education from the teeming life around us that causes a great deal of difficulty. I would not want to be incarcerated in a training college. Equally, I should have experienced work in the industrial sense.

In the years following the Second World War the Emergency Training Scheme injected a new breed of teachers into our schools. The experience of that scheme needs to be looked at again. It is not enough to have courses in sociology, social psychology and psycho-linguistics. There needs to be a knowledge gained from contact with real people in real situations.

Today, after 25 years as a professional educationist, I can survey my own knowledge and attempt to assess its validity. I am conscious that I have been conditioned to abstract myself from people. I observe, classify, and make decisions. Jim is emotionally disturbed—avoid undue pressure. Dick is having trouble with phonics—try him on the tape-recorder. Mary is not being creative—give her some stimulation. Jane spends too much time on mathematics—encourage her interests towards English.

At one level all this indicates an interest in children. It is an attempt to individualise instruction in the classroom. It is not a bad approach, yet something is lacking. That vague something is a feel for children in a way that establishes a growing relationship. I suspect that when I have succeeded I have added this human

dimension to my professionalism. This ability to establish relationships with pupils is often regarded as a gift. You either have it or
you don't. Whether this is true or not, the attitudes towards
teaching that develop during training can either foster or inhibit
this capability.

It is my contention that a great deal of present training could
inhibit the growth of those personal attitudes in teachers that are
essential if the majority of children in our classrooms are to feel
comfortable and accepted.

If we accept the evidence that Jim and Sandra have given us,
then arrogance is one prevailing characteristic that separates
teacher and child. I am a teacher and I must be right. I am a
teacher and I have authority. I am suggesting that by widening the
personal life of teachers in training the possibility is created of
fostering more liberal attitudes. I would insist that knowing
children is the foundation of good teaching. I would also insist
that one only gets to know children in a very superficial way if
one's horizon is limited to the classroom.

I am also conscious that one important aspect of my training
was the growth of myself as a person. Looking back, I can scarcely
remember the tutorials when we explored the wisdom of
Shakespeare, Froebel, Freud, Spearman, and Hughes and Hughes.
Perhaps our highly verbal abstractions were significant at the
time. Today, memory is dim.

What I do remember is the informal evening with a wise tutor,
when silence often taught more than conversation, when we
strove to understand ourselves, our job, and our purpose. I was
lucky. What I would advocate today is a greater emphasis in
colleges on self-development, not merely through study, but
through rigorous self-examination. Combine this with a wider
experience of people and academic study becomes viable.

It is study for the sake of study that breeds arrogance. It is study
and experience in a genuine search for understanding that breeds
humility.

We began with Jim and Sandra and it is with them we shall
end. It is easy to say that youngsters like them come from homes
that do not prepare them for school. They were not ready to

compete in the educational rat-race with any real chance of success. They started a sprint with one leg tied to the ground. It is less pleasant to suggest that we, the teachers, were not ready to meet their needs, or help them with their problems. Our vision was limited by the blinkers our training had forced upon us. We were taught to select and reject on our own élitist criteria.

If all Jim has gained from his schooling is a consolidation of his own prejudices, and a belief that he is rejected, then it might have been better if the whole sorry operation had never started. If all Sandra has gained from her schooling is a dream that two A-levels are a passport to fame, and a belief that by proving herself she has beaten the system, then we have served her ill. She has only gained that very arrogance she has set herself to defeat.

We must think again.

6 Children talking about teachers

Maureen O'Connor

Teachers do not, on the whole, much want to know what children think of them. 'Give them a chance to criticise their elders, to give their own opinions, and you always end up with sex, drugs and permissiveness,' said one during a hostile discussion in Sussex on a drama project. The notion which aroused so much hostility was that children should be asked to write about their own lives for a musical. Such a revolutionary idea, the teachers thought, might lead to criticism of schools or staff, and so to disciplinary problems.

And that, in a nutshell, explains why teachers know so little about what their own pupils think of them, and why, even when this book was being discussed, there was some hostile reaction to the idea of a chapter on *children*'s attitudes, as if they had no relevance at all to the educational process.

Naturally enough, children do have very pronounced views on their schools and on their teachers, and although the profession has done a pretty effective job in building a barrier high enough to exclude serious consideration of the opinions of the 'consumer' of education, there have been researchers diligent enough to attempt to find out what schoolchildren do think of their compulsory schooling.

Not all the attitudes which have been revealed are especially flattering to the teaching profession. And if teachers are honest, and keep their ears open in school, they must know that some children, in some schools, hold them in hatred, ridicule and contempt. Some form of professional conspiracy leads them to ignore this, and in putting up a barrier of silence they unfortunately exclude some of the constructive, as well as the destructive, criticism which bubbles away below them.

Children are at school for at least ten years of their lives. During that time their reactions to their teachers change from the childish awe of the five-year-old encountering its first figure of authority outside the home, to the relatively mature assessments of the school-leaver, able to compare the good teacher with the bad and back up his judgement with reasonably sophisticated argument.

It is reasonable enough perhaps to disregard the likes and dislikes of the eight-year-old in school, the child who is still capable of being surprised that his teacher leads a normal life in a normal family outside school hours. It is more arrogant to dismiss the criticisms of the fifth- or sixth-former as uninformed. How much more experience does one need before one is qualified to judge? There will not be much more, in fact, from the point of view of the pupil.

The reactions of secondary school children to their teachers vary just as much as their aptitudes and abilities do. Many appear to be completely at ease in, and satisfied with, the school situation. Others are, as any educational welfare officer will testify, so irrevocably antagonistic to school and to teachers that it is an effort to persuade them to attend at all.

But when the Schools Council conducted a major survey on the attitudes of school leavers it found that even where there was hostility many of the comments made by the more disgruntled pupils were constructive. Often the older secondary school child is, it appears, only too well aware of how well or badly he is being taught. These children—all of them early leavers, and amongst the least academic in the secondary school system— complained equally of teachers who bored them by going too slowly or who lost them by racing ahead too quickly. Almost a fifth of them made detailed criticisms of the ways in which they had been taught, many of them saying that they had not been expected to take an active enough part in their lessons.

Educationists would soon recognise in their comments opposition to the traditional 'chalk and talk' method of teaching. Comments such as 'We just sit there and read like stuffed dummies', or 'It was all notes', or 'We don't have enough discussions' echo very closely indeed the sort of criticism of traditional teaching methods which has been made within the teaching profession itself now for some time. The only 'shocking' element in these comments on poor teaching methods is that they come from the children who have suffered them.

Another area in which adolescents have strong views is over the usefulness, or otherwise, of school subjects. This is an area in which teachers can justifiably argue that pupils may be too immature and inexperienced to realise the significance of what they are learning and that they will not fully appreciate its value until long after they have left school. This can be a valid argument: it can also be an excuse for forcing children to sit through lessons they find boring instead of looking for a means of making the subject-matter interesting.

In any event, Peter Wilmott's survey of Adolescent Boys in East London (Institute of Community Studies) showed clearly enough that many boys felt that their school courses had been of little use to them. And it was the least able who showed the least enthusiasm for their school work and felt they had gained least benefit from it. Some of the secondary modern school boys saw the advantages of technical courses but they often failed to see the relevance of even the most basic academic subjects, such as English and maths, to the rest of their lives. And in areas where some interest could have been roused relatively easily, in music for instance, the schools appeared to have made very little impact.

When it came to the teachers themselves, the East End boys could not summon up much enthusiasm. A fifth of them said that they had liked few of their schoolteachers and the main complaint was that they were 'too distant'. 'You can't class them as people,' said one 15-year-old. 'You can only class them as someone in charge of you.' Others complained that their teachers had lacked patience, could not be bothered to explain difficult points in lessons, and rewarded slowness with 'a clip round the earhole'. Others commented on social differences between teachers and children, feeling that if teachers did not live in the same area as their students they were not likely to understand or sympathise with them.

This evidence is backed up by another survey on early leavers by Joan Maizels, of Bedford College, who also concluded that many youngsters left school pretty unfavourably impressed by the education they had been offered. Her group of youngsters complained about lack of encouragement at school: less than a third of them felt that their teachers had listened to what they wanted to say at school, had praised them when they did well or had even been pleasant to them. Even fewer thought that their teachers had been good to work for, clever, reliable or sincere.

Many of these children had left school as fast as possible and Miss Maizels concluded that this was because of a real dislike of school rather than the attraction of going to work. School was widely regarded as a form of captivity, with petty rules and unsympathetic staff, from which they were only too glad to escape.

Now it could be argued that to present a group of adolescents with a list of bad qualities and invite them to attach them to teachers would lead to about as unfavourable an assessment of the teaching profession as it is possible to get. But in fact most of the surveys which have been done compare very well: they all point to the fact that about a fifth of secondary school children are, on their own admission, bored, indifferent or actively hostile to school.

This heartily dissatisfied proportion is, of course, the least academically inclined, the least amenable to discipline, the group which is sure it has failed in the middle-class meritocracy from the age of 11, if not sooner. They are the ones likely to be in the bottom streams of streamed schools, or, in remedial classes, the ones likely to be truants, delinquents and trouble-makers of one sort and another: the conscientious teacher's nightmare and the reason why so many of the profession oppose the raising of the school-leaving age.

Nevertheless, these children, who realise only too clearly that they are at the bottom of the heap, socially and academically, seem to resent one thing more than anything else. This is the fact that, as they see it, their teachers are also failing them. Their criticisms are in many ways acute, and touch on many of the solutions which are being widely discussed within the profession itself: the need for more vocational courses for the non-academic child, the need for project work instead of repetitive note-taking, and the need for the establishment of good relationships with even the most difficult children. They can not only recognise that their education is not what it should be but also some of the ways in which it could be relatively easily improved.

Of course, teachers are not alone responsible for the hostile attitudes which a large minority of schoolchildren have towards their education. In working-class areas society itself, and especially the family, reinforces some children's negative feelings about education almost from the cradle. Even where parents are not actively hostile to the school—and every teacher knows of the mother or father who will come dashing into school threatening court action, or even a good thumping, for the teacher who had the temerity to punish a child—there is often a scarcely veiled contempt in working-class communities for the teaching profession. As they say in the North of England, a teacher is a man among lads and a lad among men: not much encouragement there for any self-respecting lad to continue his education beyond the legal minimum.

Hostility, contempt and sheer apathy may feed a child's own resentment of authority, and he may find his attitudes further strengthened by cultural influences. In children's comics, especially of the more old-fashioned kind favoured by small boys, teachers are invariably portrayed as ugly, vicious and even stupid. It's easy enough, perhaps, to laugh off the old comic image of Mr Quelch, sadistically wielding his cane, where there is some other image to counter-balance the satire. But there must be many homes, especially in the most deprived areas where education is in any case not highly prized, where Mr Quelch and his like, cane at the ready, are passed on from generation to generation as the teacher caricature in the forefront of children's minds.

The teacher-pupil relationship at its best is not an easy one to portray; the worst aspects of the relationship are only too easy to mock and make fun of. Certainly in the mass media the positive aspects of teaching do not get much of a look in. Stories about schools in the popular papers more often than not emphasise conflict between teachers and pupils over such petty issues as long hair or mini skirts. The film *Kes*, which included a remarkably sensitive study of one teacher's relationship with a young boy, nevertheless reduced the rest of the school staff to pretty unsympathetic caricatures. And on television the series 'Please Sir', which portrays a secondary modern school, perpetuates the idea that staff and children are involved in some sort of semi-serious war between the generations.

All this may not matter much for the child from a home where learning is encouraged, where an interest is taken in his school work, and where teachers are regarded by the parents as allies rather than enemies. But that hostile fifth of the nation's schoolchildren is far more likely to come from areas of poor housing, of problem families and low incomes, from homes where there are no books and education is regarded as a waste of time, and where the school far from being supported by the home is more likely to be actively undermined by parental attitudes which are against education and against authority in all its forms.

It is a working-class problem. Middle-class families may have teachers as neighbours, as friends or even as relatives. There is tacit support in middle-class communities for the idea that education is 'a good thing' and that passing the 11-plus and gaining some O- and A-levels are worthwhile goals. This sort of attitude just does not extend right down to the bottom of the social spectrum, and it must, in fact, be difficult sometimes for teachers, who have themselves been successful in the educational rat race, to recognise that there are areas where the community simply does not value education in the same way as they do.

In some working-class areas teachers are quite simply regarded as another branch of 'Them', and the difference between 'Us' and 'Them' is accentuated by differences of accent and social class, and by the fact, noticed by those East End boys interviewed for the

Institute of Community Studies, that teachers often live some distance from schools in poor areas. What teachers face in this sort of situation is not the hostility of children alone: it is the hostility of entire families, and even entire communities. To overcome this sort of opposition during the relatively short time a child is in school is a problem indeed.

Not that teachers do not help to build up resentments themselves inside the schools. It cannot all be blamed on outside forces for which schoolteachers have no responsibility. There is, for instance, the whole business of the 11-plus—happily abolished now in many areas but still leaving behind it a pool of resentment amongst those who 'failed'—and streaming.

It has been argued recently that however much you mix children up in school classrooms they will in effect stream themselves, that in fact they can work out very accurately how well they are doing within their group by the simple expedient of going through the class and saying 'Sam is a better reader than I am, but Jane is not as good'. Upon which basis it could be argued that all the fuss about streaming was so much hot air: children will grade themselves even in the most unstreamed school.

But this misses the point. What causes so much unhappiness in streamed schools, and in areas where there is still an 11-plus allocation of school places, is the formality of the acknowledgement of success or failure. The secondary modern school child is publicly acknowledged as 'a failure' in a race in which he is hardly old enough to know he is running. And in the strictly streamed school the relentless averaging of marks, perhaps confirmed by notices on the board and annual, or termly, promotions and demotions, makes it all too clear which is the top and which is the bottom of the ladder.

If the entire system is geared to grading children like apples is it any wonder that those at the bottom of the heap should resent the sense of total failure they are left with? Can teachers really be surprised that in the D streams of our secondary modern and comprehensive schools morale is poor, discipline is tenuously maintained, and absenteeism as common. These are the children who resent the teaching profession very bitterly. 'We are not brainy', they say and they hate the teachers who tell them so almost every day of their school lives.

A growing problem in a multiracial society is the resentment which is sometimes felt by coloured children towards their teachers because they feel that they are prejudiced against them. In an admittedly subjective report on the situation in the Handsworth area of Birmingham, Augustine John reported that some children felt that their teachers were openly hostile towards them. Other groups of immigrant youngsters will even name instances and individual teachers in their complaints of prejudice.

Obviously, this is another aspect of the 'Us' and 'Them' problem of the deprived areas, and one which it is particularly difficult for a white teacher to break down. He is quite patently even less one of the immigrant community than he is one of the white working-class community and the battle to overcome the suspicion of some of his pupils will be that much harder. But with the terrifying example of America before us it seems absolutely vital that racial suspicion should not be added to class suspicion in British schools. Immigrant children, above all, should be helped to feel that their teachers are on their side.

So far it has appeared that hostility and resentment of teachers might be confined to the 'bottom' segment of schoolchildren, the non-academics and early leavers, the drop-outs and the maladjusted, who are labelled failures at school and continue to be labelled failures in a wider society for the rest of their lives. But in one aspect of anti-teacher feeling this distinction is not quite so easy to make as it used to be. It is not only the disruptive and bloody-minded members of the D streams who resent some aspects of school discipline and authority. The resentment is spreading.

Possibly as a result of more flexible teaching methods in the primary schools, or possibly because of the more permissive approach to upbringing of many modern parents, schoolchildren are becoming increasingly critical of some aspects of school life, and amongst the most critical are the traditionally amenable members of the 'top streams', the bright children studying for O-levels and A-levels and intent on university or college places.

These erstwhile conformists, prefects and team leaders and editors of school magazines, are now often found voicing extremely articulate complaints about the way we run our schools.

The hostility of organisations such as the Schools Action Union is not directed at teachers as such, but it is opposed to some of the more unhallowed practises which they endorse. One of the main planks of their platform is the abolition of corporal punishment, and there have been a significant number of cases recently involving the refusal of pupils to accept this kind of chastisement. There have been other, well-publicised battles over what large numbers of children seem to regard as petty regulations, over dress and hair length, over pop music or the publication of 'obscene' or simply critical articles in school magazines.

To some extent this is merely a reflection of the traditional conflict between the generations. The revolt against parental authority has always been reflected in even the most academic schools. What is new in the present wave of revolts and demonstrations is the beginning of an interschool organisation to co-ordinate the movement for specific reforms, and the use of publications, such as the *Little Red School Book*, to spread the new gospel.

What has happened is that the usual disgruntled resentment of the non-academic secondary school boy or girl against such irritants as school uniform, the cane, and some of the school rules, has been taken up by a much wider spectrum of youngsters in the heady name of 'freedom'. In many ways teachers themselves have encouraged this new independence of thought but they have not yet come to terms with it, at least in the average secondary school community.

Meanwhile the children's attitudes are hardening as they realise that they are not alone. They have always appreciated teachers who are fair and are seen to be fair: they are now becoming increasingly interested in rules which are fair and which can be genuinely justified by the interests of the smooth running of a large institution. They are increasingly resentful of what they regard as infringements of their personal liberty, whether it is in decrees on the length of their hair or in the infliction of physical punishment.

To some extent this is still just an extension of the traditional battle between the generations, taken one stage further by a more self-confident group of teenagers than have gone before. But perhaps the battle moves to a new plane when teenagers begin to ask for the same freedoms inside school that they see adults enjoying outside: freedom of speech, for instance, and an element of democracy in the running of the school. This is a major change in attitude and one which, if not handled tactfully, could spread hostility towards teachers from the traditional 'hard core' of difficult children to a much wider spectrum of bright and highly articulate teenage pupils.

It is, of course, naïve to expect any school system to exist without building up resentments of some sort in some of the pupils. Compulsory education can hardly be organised at all without some form of authoritarianism, subtly disguised as it may be. But what seems to be happening in some schools at the moment is that the natural resentment of children towards authority is being unnecessarily accentuated by unfairnesses within the system. A normal child will inevitably come to terms with rules if he can see their point and justification. A child from a caring home and a belief in the value of education will in any case put up with unfairness at school because he can see the long-term benefits of sticking it out. Where conflict exists in school it is inevitably again the child from the worst home background, with the least incentive to persevere, who will come off worst.

In the past teachers have not been required to justify their actions. Their word, inside the school walls, has been law. Today children are demanding justice, whether it is over minor matters of dress and personal appearance—why can a teacher grow his hair long if a pupil can't?—or major issues—why should teachers be able to get away with discrimination, or inflict physical punishment, when such actions are illegal outside school? These are the sort of resentments which add fuel to any teenage rebellion. Add them to a sense of failure and inadequacy and they may turn the least able child into an unteachable one. Such children are lost prematurely to the educational system. They may not come to school at all, if they can get away with it, and they leave school officially as soon as they legally can. All one can ask is whether it is the resentful and hostile child who has failed or whether it is the system.

If about a fifth of the country's secondary school children are basically hostile to school and to most of their teachers—and some teachers, especially those who oppose the raising of the school-leaving age, would argue that the proportion is even higher in some difficult schools—then clearly something is radically wrong somewhere. Children are not born with a preconceived hatred of all things educational. They pick it up somewhere along the way between being fairly open minded and amenable five-year-old entrants and totally recalcitrant 15-year-old early leavers.

Partly it may be bred by the appalling environment in which so many children have to live, by squalid housing conditions, by family stress and violence which stunt the emotions and warp the mind. Partly it is bred within the schools by physical conditions, by overcrowded classes and overworked teachers. And yet—it does not happen to every child from a poor environment who attends a 'slum' school. There are teachers, and it would be foolish to describe them as saints, although they are remarkable, who seem to be able to make progress in the most deprived areas with the most maladjusted children. Some teachers do seem to be able to break down the hostility and resentment of the least able child and build in its place something worthy of the name of education.

Less exceptional teachers need more help, and the lines that help should develop along are already fairly clear. Many schools are beginning to recognise the vital importance of the home-school relationship. They see that parents must be persuaded of the value of what the schools have to offer if they are to avoid the situation in which school and family pull a child in different directions. The use of school counsellors as a link between school and home, and as advisers with a specific responsibility for a child's welfare, is a recognition that many classroom difficulties have their roots outside the school.

The colleges of education, too, are beginning to recognise that social studies have a direct relevance to the teacher's function and this is an area where the trainers specifically could make a major contribution to solving the problem of intractable youngsters in the secondary schools. But the colleges will have to move faster than they have done so far if their commitment is to be taken seriously.

But perhaps of even greater significance would be some sort of effort to dissipate the feelings of failure which dog so many schoolchildren. It may be difficult for teachers, who have been extremely successful themselves in academic terms, to acknowledge that there are other goals in education than examination successes. But this is what they must do if they are to help the children who will never pass examinations. It is significant that London's big new comprehensive schools have had considerable success in persuading children to stay at school longer. They appear to be large enough, and to offer a sufficiently large range of courses, to overcome the urge of at least some potentially hostile children to leave at the earliest possible moment. Presumably they are able to persuade most of their pupils that they can succeed, at least to some extent, at *something*.

The effect of changes in discipline is less easy to measure, although an increasing number of schools are finding that they can survive without the use of corporal punishment. Certainly it is time for teachers to look carefully at those aspects of school organisation which clash most blatantly with the freedom teenagers are now given outside school. Should sanctions as severe as suspension be used in cases involving what are, after all, merely matters of personal taste? Would discipline really break down if girls were allowed to dress in the latest fashion inside school as well as outside, or boys allowed to express their growing masculinity in the classroom as well as on the sportsfield? Some of the conflicts between teachers and schoolchildren occasionally give the impression that teachers are positively courting the dislike of their adolescent charges.

Hostility in school, though, is not a trivial problem. Antagonistic teenagers, big and possibly violent, can terrorise a class and even a teacher, making genuine teaching almost impossible. The difficulties of trying to teach in one of our 'down-town' secondary schools should not be minimised. And yet the reaction of those teachers who feel that these most troublesome children should be encouraged to get out of school as soon as possible is a counsel of despair. Every child has the right to expect an equal amount of effort on his part, however troublesome he may be. Yet even that champion of the deprived, Sir Alec Clegg, has warned that the discipline problem may get completely out of hand after the raising of the school-leaving age if some way is not found to arouse the interest and enthusiasm of the 'anti-school' child who is now to stay on yet a year longer.

In such a crisis even unpalatable solutions may have to be considered, as unpalatable as the changes in systems of grading, or of school discipline I have suggested. In addition there may well have to be a change in attitude on the part of teachers themselves, a change so great that it can probably only come by a broadening of the pattern of training in the colleges.

In so many respects teachers at present appear to be breeding the very resentments in children which cause so much trouble in the classroom. Ironically, if they only felt able to relax their traditional conception of discipline enough to ask their 'clients' *why* they are so dissatisfied with the service they are being offered they might hear something to their advantage. Far from wanting to over-throw the schools the children want to improve them: and they have a pretty fair idea of how to set about it, too, if only someone would listen.

7 What is wrong with the three-year course

Michael Storm

Everyone knows exactly what is wrong with the teacher-training course. And that is the problem. Teachers know that it should be much more practical, more down-to-earth, with greater emphasis on lesson planning, class management; there is no substitute, they say, for direct classroom experience—shop-floor, coal-face, are favourite ways of conveying the gritty actuality that is required. Sometimes these sentiments have curious historical echoes. After all, it is not so very long since elementary school teachers served a sort of craft apprenticeship, on the job, without any nonsense about colleges and professional training.

The 1944 McNair Committee was equally certain about what was wrong. The committee saw the low status of elementary school teachers as being due to their own very modest educational attainments, and recommended that student-teachers should not be deprived of personal higher education. The McNair remedy was to add the study of one or two subjects 'in depth' to the existing low-level mixture of helpful tips, basketwork and general interest courses. Hence the 'main subject' which is one of the few features of the teacher-training curriculum to occur with some consistency in almost all of the astonishingly diverse 164 colleges.

But a third group strongly questions the value of this main subject strand, often invoking the mystically powerful term 'relevance'. They would like to see much more differentiation within teacher-training courses. For example, there would be no main subject requirement for infant teachers and a good deal of it for secondary teachers. On the other hand, educationists stress that on entry students cannot be expected to know which age group they would like to teach, and must be given the opportunity of sampling a variety of teaching situations. In any case, it is argued, it is important for the junior teacher, during her training, to have some experience of infant work, and for the secondary teacher to know what goes on in the primary school.

More significantly, the N.U.T. lends its support to this argument, largely because it fears that more differentiated courses within the colleges would create an undersirable hierarchical structure within the ranks of certified teachers, cutting infant teachers off from further academic qualifications and restricting mobility. The N.U.T. is strongly attached to the notion of 'the general teacher', an awe-inspiring figure 'who can adapt himself to the changing nature and needs of children in varying age ranges, in depressing or congenial surroundings, and who can, in any one of these situations, satisfy the needs and demands of the differing children who make up the class'. (*Teacher education—the way ahead*, N.U.T., 1970). This implies a relatively undifferentiated course.

We have not yet exhausted the list of those who know what is wrong with teacher training. There are those who regard it as vital that all trainee teachers should be competent to operate and maintain all forms of audio-visual equipment, to practise counselling skills with problem children, to teach about sex, to foster international and interracial understanding, to run group therapy sessions, to conduct outdoor environmental investigations, to use programmed learning techniques, to possess a basic core of librarianship skills—and so on.

Then there are those who deplore the lack of communication between educational researchers and practising teachers, and see the colleges as the channel through which intending teachers should come to understand the language (largely statistical) and techniques of educational research, as well as its recent findings. No student should leave without knowing about regression analysis.

This pressure is matched by those who stress the 'pastoral' rôle of the institution, and the need for the student to be able to identify with a single experienced tutor who will be understanding and sympathetic towards her problems. Such a tutor, sometimes unkindly termed a 'mother hen', may lack expertise in psychology, sociology, or educational research methods, but compensates for these deficiencies by offering wise personal guidance.

Another opinion, represented by the Society for the Promotion of Educational Reform through Teacher Training, would like the colleges to place much less emphasis on supplying existing schools with young teachers trained to work within the existing pattern. A college should rather be a revolutionary enclave within the education system, sending out tough ideologues energetically hostile to established patterns, whether staffroom hierarchies, selection systems, curriculum content or examining methods. One might link with this the pressure upon the colleges to recognise, in their training courses, a necessary extension of the teacher's rôle to that of unofficial social welfare and community relations worker; certainly teacher training has always had a strong missionary flavour.

Then there are those who believe that the age and inexperience of the students stringently limits what can be accomplished in any initial training course, despite the fruitless attempts to produce the fully-equipped professional teacher. Much more emphasis should be placed, they say, on extending to student teachers a good post-A-level general education, with massive investment in in-service training programmes which would be far more effective, involving dialogue rather than indoctrination.

All these recipes for improving the college course are impeccably motivated and powerfully substantiated. I have listed them in an attempt to illustrate that there is no consensus of opinion on teacher training. This would not matter were it not for the fact that the colleges are notoriously 'liberal' institutions. Buffeted by gales of exhortation from every side—and from within, for the staffs of colleges are remarkably heterogeneous—the colleges display a liberal reluctance to exclude anything which might be of value. Courses grow by accretion, as attempts are made to placate each new pressure group, to accommodate yet more desirable functions. The result is what a young teacher recently termed 'the butterfly day'.

The week's time-table of a hypothetical college student would demonstrate clearly the result of all these conflicting pressures. On Monday morning he attends a lecture by a guest speaker on smoking and lung cancer. Afterwards he manages to complete an essay on *Huckleberry Finn*, part of an assignment issued in a curricular English course. In the afternoon there is a lecture on educational psychology, part of his education course. In the evening he prepares two wall-charts for use on Tuesday, when his morning is spent in a primary school. Here he makes notes while the headmaster describes the evolution of the parent-teacher association and its fund-raising activities. Later he meets a class of eight-year-olds. On Tuesday afternoon he takes part in an improvisation session, part of a curricular drama course, in which he does his best to simulate the behaviour of an anguished Vietnamese refugee.

Wednesday is his main subject day; in the morning he reads a paper on the Munich crisis to a small group of fellow history students. He enjoyed preparing this assignment, but has to acknowledge the tutor's gentle criticism that he has used a very restricted range of secondary sources. The tutor's attempts to stimulate discussion are not very successful, since the other students have read even less, and are naturally reluctant to reveal this. In the afternoon, together with other students, he works on a display of teaching materials on Travel in Medieval Times. Some time is wasted when the supply of sugar paper runs out.

Thursday morning finds him at the Town Hall, waiting to see the housing manager; this is part of an assignment in the sociology component of the education course. After lunch he searches in the library for books on West Africa, as he has decided to take 'Slavery' as his main theme in a forthcoming teaching practice. He is scheduled to meet his supervisor for a preliminary discussion of this practice, but as he has never met her before—she is a biology lecturer—he has some difficulty finding her room, only to find that she has gone to a workshop on the new primary mathematics, held for interested colleagues by the college mathematics department.

On Friday morning he joins another group of students on a

curricular music course, and learns a good deal about how to make percussion instruments from kitchen debris. He manages to fit in a staff-student committee meeting, where ways of measuring, and possibly reducing, the student work-load are discussed, before hurrying off to the regular weekly meeting with his personal tutor, who communicates to him a list of forthcoming college events (notice-boards are deemed to be too impersonal and ineffectual) and hopefully enquires whether he has any problems.

This is not an exaggerated portrait. My own college has steadily reduced the input of separate components in the course but there is still a period in the first year when students may be engaged upon a dozen different strands of study. Notice that this is not a particularly unpleasant week; most of the activities are enjoyable, and all of them could be justified by one or more of the arguments reviewed earlier. It is, however, likely to be deficient in both intellectual satisfaction and vocational efficiency, for it is impossibly fragmented.

The college course is generally labelled 'concurrent', to describe the parallel pursuit of 'professional' and 'personal' education. But this term inadequately conveys the real diversity involved. The education course will involve both school-based work and highly theoretical studies; curricular courses range uneasily along the spectrum between content and method—for it's difficult to discuss optimum ways of using, say, poetry in the classroom if the student has no personal resources or enthusiasms in this area: whilst main subject courses frequently involve a professional concern for teaching themes, problems and materials within the chosen area, as well as offering the student the opportunity of advanced study at his own level.

Does the resultant fragmentation really matter? After all, it is not particularly new. The colleges have always attempted to turn out 'the well-rounded, versatile person'; criticisms of the standards of primary teaching have often been, by implication, criticisms of the colleges' traditional concern for the type of low-level omnicompetence believed to be an appropriate attribute for the teacher of young children.

In an attempt to remedy deplorably low standards in the teaching of reading or mathematics, art or history, science or environmental studies, intensive in-service courses are often organised. If one talks to young teachers attending such courses, it is clear that their colleges generally *did* offer training in the area now revealed as weak. But the training was so compressed, so crowded in with a host of other 'vital' courses—and so inevitably remote from the urgency of the need to provide regular daily sustenance for forty developing minds—that its *impact* was minimal.

I believe that the ineffectual diffusion of student energies occasioned by the present concurrent pattern is the principal weakness of the college course. This diffusion contributes towards an immense 'credibility gap'. The existence of this gap may be demonstrated in a variety of ways. The course, as impressively described in the college prospectuses, requires the student to engage—often simultaneously—in the study of sociology, psychology, philosophy, the structure and evolution of the English schools system, and a major academic discipline which he may take to B.Ed. level. In addition, he will be required to equip himself with a battery of skills in teaching a variety of other subjects, and he will need to demonstrate his competence in extended periods of practical teaching. The successful completion of such a programme would appear to call for quite exceptional intellectual powers. Yet the evidence suggests that entrants to colleges of education are not of the highest academic calibre, however this is measured.

Perhaps the most striking illustrations of this come from the comments of head teachers 'supporting' their sixth-form applicants: 'He is of limited academic ability with a record of laziness and lack of effort ... although on his academic performance he is a very marginal candidate, he is well worth consideration for a place in a college of education.' Some comments are more enthusiastic: 'It is to be expected that his personal qualities will make him acceptable as a teacher in situations where academic achievement is not necessary.'

Many sixth-formers one interviews are clearly regarding teacher training as a poor second to a university place. Of more than 54,000 who applied for college places in 1970, over 13,000 withdrew their applications, mainly because they had gained admittance to an institution possessing higher status. Formal entry qualifications are low; a recent survey* showed that more than two-thirds of students entering universities have A-levels equivalent to three 'Cs' or better, whilst the figure for colleges of education is one-twentieth. It is extremely difficult to fail to gain admission to a college course, and many colleges are hardly in a position to *select* their intake at all. The A.T.C.D.E. point out that 'over the last ten years the quality of the intake to the colleges has declined relative to the improved attainments of school leavers'.†

Of course, A-levels are not everything, but it does seem odd that students whose successes in organised study have been relatively slender should be offered the rich and demanding programme represented by the concurrent course. One might reasonably suppose that some of them would find such a course too demanding, and consequently fail to achieve a satisfactory standard.

But here the credibility gap widens further. If it is difficult to fail to get into a college, it is even more difficult to fail the course. 'An eventual failure rate of under two students in every hundred, and in-course wastage for all reasons, personal, domestic, and academic, running at just over six per cent, means that the vast majority of those who are offered a college place, and virtually all those who manage to occupy it for the full three years, are assured of qualified status.'‡ It is true that the colleges are increasingly concerned about the rising rate of in-course withdrawals. But most of these are, one suspects, rejecting the college course, rather than being rejected by it. A letter from a student withdrawing midway through her first year makes the point succinctly: 'Rather than spend three years aiming for a teaching certificate which will not qualify me for any other career, I have decided that I ought to aim at a degree.'

Perhaps the worst effect of the inflated and tangled nature of the

* Noel Entwhistle of Lancaster University.
† A.T.C.D.E. 1971, *The Professional Education of Teachers*.
‡ William Taylor, *Societies and the Education of Teachers*, Faber 1969.

D

concurrent course is the mood of scepticism which tends to set in, once the students realise that book lists and study assignments are part of an amiable charade. The concurrent course is particularly frustrating for the more able student, who is offered a series of superficial introductory glimpses of areas of study. He is allowed to penetrate far enough to become interested, yet not far enough to achieve anything; in the context of a college tutorial, he realises, intellectual eminence may be won by the perusal of a single paperback or article.

For the tutors, pressure of time, a sense of competing for the interest and attention of students, and, sometimes, an almost evangelical fervour that students should emerge with 'the right attitudes' can lead to a compressed, dehydrated course-content. Polarities are established ('formal' versus 'informal', 'integrated' versus 'subject-centred') and complex ideas become slogans ('child-centredness', 'reading-readiness', 'learning through experience'). Students gain a fairly clear notion of the sorts of teaching procedures that are currently approved, but often have a less confident grasp of the educational theory that justifies the procedures. As Jerome Bruner puts it, 'There is a lack of an integrating theory in pedagogy . . . in its place there is principally a body of maxims.'*

From the teaching of reading to curriculum reform in secondary schools, the world of education is a world of problems, issues, arguments; yet one would hardly suspect this from the placid atmosphere of the college of education, where conflicts dissolve in a diffused sweetness and light. Of course, the development of argument takes longer than the assimilation of a vague conventional wisdom, a Victorian onwards-and-upwards ethos. Here again the concurrent course is unhelpful, ensuring that young teachers are often ill-equipped to participate in the swirling controversies of the outside world.

The superficial nature of many of the studies undertaken by college students is nowhere more vividly revealed than by the swift subsequent erosion of the educational attitudes inculcated by the college. One can see this process at work well before the end of

* *Towards a Theory of Instruction*, Harvard University Press 1966.

the course. The same student who is undoubtedly submitting essays about the problems of the disadvantaged adolescent, will comment quite naturally about pupils being 'appallingly thick'.

In some respects, the colleges resemble elaborate primary schools with adult pupils. William Taylor notes as a major characteristic of the colleges, 'a suspicion of the intellect and the intellectual'. There is a commitment to 'the belief that the approach matters more than the content, that understanding is more important than facts'. Note here the significant use of polarised categories, what Dewey called 'the Either-Or mode of thinking'. Can one understand anything without knowing something about it?

If we add to this a preoccupation with pastoral or therapeutic rôles in relation to the student, evidenced by a widespread reluctance to introduce objective assessments 'which may conflict with the best interests of the student',* we can see some basis for Professor Bantock's claim that the colleges maintain 'an anaemic and claustrophobic pastoralism, with a lack of intellectual rigour and liveliness'.

The ill-defined and multiplying objectives of the concurrent course have always posed considerable problems in staff recruitment. Great emphasis is placed upon extensive school experience, yet this is not always easily distilled and communicated in the form of substantial courses. The university authorities which validate college certificate and B.Ed. qualifications are inclined to look askance at non-graduate tutors handling courses on developmental psychology, learning theory, or comparative education. Similarly, practising teachers are sceptical of the credentials of tutors highly qualified in sociology, physics, or theology, but with little or no primary school experience, supervising students working in this sector. The ideal college lecturer would appear to require a formidable blend of experience and qualifications.

College of education work is quite unlike any other type of higher education teaching in the diversity of the demands made

* J. N. Morris, Article in *The Teacher*, 6 March 1970.

upon the lecturer. New staff may have invaluable school experience, or bring important academic expertise, but by definition
they will have had little or no experience of working with the
18–21 age group (not to mention mature students). It is often
forgotten that the massive expansion of the colleges (more than
trebling their student numbers during the last decade) has meant a
proportionately large inflow of new staff, so that in new and
rapidly expanding colleges it can be exceptional to find many
lecturers with more than five years experience.

College lecturers have remarkable autonomy in the design and
assessment of courses—at least compared with the secondary
sector. Indeed almost any form of human activity will be found,
somewhere, legitimised as a college of education course. This
autonomy, combined with the relative inexperience of many
college staff, has inevitably meant that any student moving
through the colleges within the last decade has spent a large
proportion of her time as a guinea-pig, on highly experimental
courses being tried out by recently appointed lecturers.

Fortunately, the traditional concurrent course, with all its inner
contradictions and outer pretensions, is not likely to survive the
current focussing of critical energies upon teacher training.
Formidable forces are arrayed against its continuance. In the first
place, there is the emerging consensus that the monotechnic
nature of teacher education has no future. The monotechnic
argument emphasises the need for future teachers to be trained in
institutions together with students on other courses, especially
those working for 'social service' qualifications—child care
officers, probation officers, and so on. The proposal has generated
wide approval but little, if any, working out of the practical
implications. There will always be far more trainee teachers than
trainee social workers; how do we distribute the courses so as to
ensure that student teachers have a suitable selection of contemporaries alongside them? There has been little assessment of
the capacity of colleges of education to operate non-teaching
courses, or the mechanism by which such courses would be
extracted from their existing well-established institutional homes
and re-planted in the colleges. Indeed it often appears that the

other students should be trained at the colleges *primarily* to improve the experience of trainee teachers, rather than because they, the social workers, would get a better course there. The argument sometimes appears to cast the 'other students' in the rôle of animated visual aids enhancing the effectiveness of teacher training.

The concurrent course might possibly survive the type of multiplication of institutional functions but the increasing reluctance of school-leavers to commit themselves, at 17 or 18, to a form of training leading to a specific, non-transferable type of qualification, is a far more serious threat to the concurrent course.

It has long been evident that many of the entrants to teacher training are using the colleges primarily as a means of access to *some* form of higher education, rather than as an avenue to teaching as a career. 'A picture emerges of a large number of reluctant teachers entering our colleges of education because they have nowhere else to go.'* The combination of increasing demand for post-school personal education, not necessarily of the conventional single-subject degree type, and a decreasing willingness to undertake narrowly vocational studies at 18, seems to indicate that a *consecutive* type of programme would be more appropriate, with a two- or three-year sequence of studies primarily concerned with personal education, followed by a one or two year professional component. The 'probationary year', now an empty ritual, would become an integral part of training, involving the use of paid 'teacher-tutors' in the schools, and in-service training would be more generously and systematically provided—and recognised for status and salary purposes.

A consecutive course would go a long way towards clarifying the objectives of the colleges' work. In part one the personal education element would be dominant. There would be a strong emphasis on student choice, on new interdisciplinary areas of study, and many students might elect to incorporate education studies in their programme. There would be a great reduction, however, in the number of parallel strands required, or permitted,

* A. Smithers and S. Carlisle, 'Reluctant Teachers' (*New Society*, 5 March 1970).

and not all students would use their part one qualification to proceed to a professional course. The status of this qualification within the currency system of higher education would need to be carefully determined.

Those students proceeding to the professional course would embark upon a highly differentiated programme, in which there would be a much closer and more continuous focussing upon the age-range and/or curriculum sector selected by the student. Parents have a right to expect that their children will be taught by well-educated people who are also professional specialists. Infant teachers will be specialists in development psychology, and the teaching of reading and numeracy; primary and middle school teachers would be equipped with a sophisticated understanding of how children learn, and with considerable expertise in one or two areas of the curriculum, so as to make an effective and distinctive contribution to the team-teaching operations increasingly favoured in these schools.

Development along these lines would have the added advantage that colleges would be able to concentrate upon particular academic strengths. One of the most embarrassing manifestations of the credibility gap stems from the small scale of many of the colleges. A college with less than 750 students will often be purporting to offer 10 or 12 subjects to B.Ed. level. This means, in effect, that in some subject areas one or two lecturers, normally with lengthy teaching experience separating them from their own university studies, will be struggling valiantly to maintain degree courses at an academically respectable level. Such colleges might choose to restrict the range of studies offered—part one of a consecutive course need no longer reflect the entire school curriculum—or to specialise in the initial training or in-service function.

The adoption of a consecutive course would ensure that the very significant contribution that the colleges have always made to the education of a large proportion (currently over 30 per cent) of those entering full-time education after 18, could be maintained and further developed. (Main subject studies are rarely the least highly regarded elements in the present concurrent course.) It is vital that this should be so, for the universities and other institutions are unlikely to be able to absorb the whole of the expanding demand for post-school general education, nor can we assume that this demand can in any way equate with a strong interest in teaching as a career.

Those who react with horror at the prospect of young people delaying their choice of a teaching career to twenty or later are really adopting a Canute-type posture. For whatever dedicated teachers may think, *a rapidly increasing proportion* of the teachers entering our schools at all levels, in the next decade, will be qualifying through the one-year post-graduate certificate course. Young women with honours degrees in classics, archaeology, or biochemistry will be taking a highly congested one-year course, and a post teaching eight-year-olds. The A.T.C.D.E. proposals at least hold out the hope of a rather more appropriate type of consecutive course than this.

8 Why I left teaching

Shirley Toulson

It is thought people stop being teachers for two main reasons: if they are women they get pregnant, and if they are men, and especially if they are male scientists, the lure of the industrial fleshpots is too strong. A more souped-up version will include scary stories of clergymen's daughters being driven to nervous breakdowns in down-town blackboard jungles.

Life is never as simple as this. People insist on being individuals, and their motives are usually highly complex, and often contradictory. The point in talking to five ex-teachers, who left the profession for apparently superficial reasons, was to try to unravel some of the more subjective forces that had finally pushed them out of the classroom; and to suggest how a different organisation of the schools, and perhaps of the initial training course, might possibly keep some of our most valuable teachers teaching.

Mary will appear as a very ordinary statistic—she left to have a baby, and is determined not to go back to work at all until her child is five. Superficially her only slight deviance is that she married late and was 35 when she became pregnant. This meant that the schools had 15 years' very successful service from her. But the really significant thing is that she is quite clear in her own mind that the pregnancy happened at the right time—she would probably have left anyway. Why?

She did her training in a small rural college of education from 1953 to 1955, where she specialised in infant and nursery work. Her probationary year was spent with a nursery class of 45 four–five-year-olds in a slum clearance area in the north-west.

She stayed there for two and a half years and finally left because the school was run on such very formal lines. Even her nursery children were strictly time-tabled and expected to do some form of examination. But even in such an unlikely set-up Mary seems to have realised her potential as an extraordinarily creative teacher of young children. With a college friend she was appointed to a new school in a new town near London. 'It was literally built around us', she remembers. After two years the school changed to a family grouping system—the first infant school in the south-east to do so.

After five years' teaching, Mary spent a year attending a university child development course, and then came her second pioneering appointment. She went to the first open-plan school and was there for three years. 'It was terribly hard work, partly because of the visitors, but there was always a very happy atmosphere between staff and children.'

When she got married in 1967—oddly enough to an engineer, not a teacher—she found the travelling too difficult and managed to change to a school nearer home. But already she was beginning to have the feeling that school was getting a bit stale, though she explained this by the fact of the novelty of the conflicting demands of running a home. Really though, she was beginning to feel that, no matter what the circumstances, 'after 15 years of school you find yourself in too narrow a world. You start attaching too much importance to little things.' She partly blamed the onset of her restlessness on the fact of having moved from a school with a mixed staff to one with an all-female staff. But by the time the baby started, she was determined that she wanted to get out of the schools, in any case, and do something completely different for a couple of years, though she didn't write off the possibility of returning after that time.

This thought having been admitted, she had also to admit that she might have left teaching a few years earlier but for the fact that she had no other training. 'You can't just be a secretary. You can't work in a shop unless you're prepared to take that sort of drop in salary, status and holidays. I didn't intend to make another career,' she says, 'I just felt the need to get a fresh outlook

—to work with adults instead of children. When you work with children for 15 years you do get a bit infantile.'

Yet she is a dedicated classroom teacher. Several times various powerful people have urged her to apply for promotion, but she always turned it down. 'I have never wanted to be a head-mistress,' she explains. 'I like being with the children. Anyway, I'm not a very methodical person, and I'd probably be hopeless at administration.' She did admit, though, that she enjoyed talking to parents, and she did think that the time had come when she would really like to be doing her own thing, rather than running other people's!

Mary's case, then, is far more about career structures than about married women wastage. Fifteen years is a long time, and no one could say that her initial two-year training was in any way wasted. But her story brings out two big questions. Can it be a good thing that teachers, however able, are forced to stay in the schools simply because their training fits them for no other work? What career prospects are there for good, imaginative pioneering classroom teachers who do not wish to turn administrators? The proper education of children demands that we find proper answers, but let no one imagine they can be simple.

Michael's reason for leaving the classroom is as conventional as Mary's. For the life he wanted for himself and his family, the money just wasn't good enough. Industry could provide him with the sort of standard of living he was looking for. But it wasn't a question of youthful idealism hardening into early-middle-aged pragmatism. He never wanted to be a teacher, and thought he would like to go into sales management. So when he left a northern university with a lower-second science degree he worked for 15 months as a trainee executive with a large firm. But he found the experience of travelling around looking at various branches of the firm, and being given neither work nor responsibility, very depressing and time-wasting. It was exaspera-tion with this situation that made him apply for a job in a Midland secondary modern school near his home.

The decision was not made completely out of the blue. His wife, who had been a qualified secretary, had left that work to take a teacher-training course, and his mother had worked as an unqualified teacher in an infant school. In any case he appeared to be a natural, and had some quite outstanding academic successes with his pupils, some of whom were taking A-level physics and maths during his four years at the school.

At first he said that he felt that it didn't matter at all that he'd never been trained for teaching, he always found himself in command of the classroom situation, 'the kids didn't dare play me up'. He taught in that school of 550 boys for four years, during part of which time he acted as head of his department. Relations at the school, although good on the whole, had their uneasy side. Non-graduates on the staff resented his graduate allowance, and there was talk about untrained teachers. Eventually he became really fed up and started searching for something else.

Looking back, he can now analyse the causes of his frustration. He remembers (and here he contradicts some of the things that he had earlier said about training) that when he first went to the school he was quite petrified, and for two weeks he just sat watching lessons from the back of the class. By the beginning of the third year he found, however, that a routine had set in, and with it came the usual measure of boredom. It was then that he began to be conscious of the low status of teachers, of the desperate feeling of isolation from the rest of the community. He is convinced that poor salaries were at the root of this. When he left teaching, then in his late twenties, he was getting £1,100 p.a. and that included his graduate allowance as well as the money for head of department post. He found that he was resenting the better-off parents; beside them he felt 'just a chalky old teacher in threadbare clothes'. The poor-relation rôle was emphasised when he was given lifts to work by sixth-formers or by his own laboratory assistant.

But money was not the whole of it. He was aware of the gap between the science he was teaching and the demands of industry. This reflected the way in which schools are cut off from the real world. Looking more closely at his own experience and that of his colleagues, he concluded that 'teachers just can't have enough experience to pass on because they haven't seen enough'. This made him worry about his responsibility to his pupils and the influence he had on them. 'Every day the only people you meet are children—so you get a false sense of righteousness—you're always right. It comes of spending day after day in a room in which you are the only specialist.'

He found himself beginning to notice 'the depressing introverts and failures on the staff—teachers who'd come into the schools because they'd failed to get the jobs they really wanted—failed initially to get into university.' Teaching became equated with 'safety'. It was the 'ever-open profession'. Even the much envied long holidays were no compensation for such a state of affairs. 'Holidays are only O.K. if you've the money to spend.'

In such a mood he wrote to every large firm offering vacancies for sales representatives, and when he left teaching he was able to walk straight into a job which paid a salary of £1,400, gave him a generous expense account, arranged a non-contributory pension scheme, renewed his car every 18 months and gave him a washing and garage allowance for it. 'And even then I was told I undersold myself.'

He has been out of teaching for nearly six years now, and although he believes today's teachers are a lot less isolated, and manage to keep in touch more with other members of the profession, he would never dream of going back. 'Some of the old restrictions could still apply.' On the day he left teaching, Michael gave a party for all his teaching friends. Many of them are still in the schools. But science teachers are so badly needed that the departure of even one of them merits some thought.

Michael's case is, of course, historical. Today no such animal exists, every graduate must have a professional training before he can be employed in the schools; and whatever may be said for or against the courses leading to the Post-graduate Certificates in Education, at least they give a person time to consider what teaching is going to mean in terms of rewards and job satisfaction. But many of his complaints are still relevant—true, salaries have improved, but they still lag a long way behind what industry can offer, and it's no use pretending that money and status are not linked. No reasonably ambitious young man is going to opt for remaining a second-class citizen if he can see a way out.

In another way, Michael's case is slightly atypical. In 1970, when the Economist Intelligence Unit prepared a report on behalf of the Association of Teachers in Colleges and Departments of Education on the remuneration of young teachers and its effect on recruitment and wastage, it was found that 'many more non-graduates than graduates were leaving because of dissatisfaction with salary or salary prospects'. Between 1965, when Michael finally left teaching, and 1970 when the E.I.U. report was prepared, teachers salaries had gone up considerably—but so had the cost of living. The report quotes a remark made by a 28-year-old non-graduate primary teacher on Scale 1 graded post of £1,400 a year. 'I enjoy teaching very much but it just goes back to simple money . . . I can see what my salary is going to be in six years' time and we just could not cope with the mortgage.'

Out of 47 interviews with men teachers who had recently left the profession, the compilers of the report found only one non-graduate who gave personal reasons as his sole reason for leaving the profession. Graduates, on the other hand, complained more about their dissatisfaction with the teaching rôle itself. But can the two matters be separated? If teachers' salaries were to be substantially increased that would so alter the position of the teacher in society that his rôle would become completely changed. Society at present lets underpaid workers toil away in semi-isolation in out-of-date buildings with poor and sparse equipment. Pay a person properly, and everyone will want to know what he's up to—the isolation which Michael so justly complained of would be ended.

Meanwhile his remark that far too many teachers have never seen enough of the outside world remains true. Should anyone be expected to spend his whole life in school with his training years as the only break? For the sake of the pupils should this state of affairs even be allowed to happen? John is still nearly 10 years off retiring age, yet he is now lecturing only part-time in a college of education because he wants to devote more time and energy to his specialised interest in contemporary literature.

He started his career by winning a state scholarship to an

Oxbridge college. At that time he had no intention of becoming a teacher, and thought that he probably wanted to be a journalist. Fate took a hand when his college scholarship came to an end in his last year, and the only way he could get the money to continue his studies was by a grant through his local education authority by the then Ministry of Education. A condition went with this money, he was bonded to teach for two years.

This was the mid-30s, and jobs even in the schools were scarce. He remembers that he applied for nearly 40 posts before he got a job. Small wonder that he views his present voluntary relinquishment of a senior post in a college of education with some astonishment. 'It's a big step for someone of my generation,' he says. 'When I started teaching, one hung on to the job.'

Like Michael, John had no actual teacher training. But he learnt one or two tricks of the trade on the way, and partly got through his probationary year by the device of having all the children put their hands up whenever he asked a question when the inspector was in the room. Only those who knew the answer, however, were allowed to put their right hands up. This doesn't prove anything about how good he was at getting facts to stick in memories, but it says a lot for the rapport he achieved with his class. This is something he was always good at. The sixth-formers he taught before he went from school to college still bring him work they've written.

His first phase of teaching ended with the war. Or perhaps one should say classroom teaching, for he served in the Army Education Corps. When he came out of the Army in 1947, however, he did not go straight back into the schools. After five years, lack of money again drove him back to the classroom, since his business was hit by the general austerity of the time. From that year, until recently, he remained in education completely, first in the schools, where he eventually became a head of department, and later in a college of education. He never had cause to regret his 10 years in the outside world, and feels that all teachers need to have at least a sabbatical year to give them a chance to get away from children and do something completely different.

He found teaching, whether pupils in school or students at

college, a completely absorbing job. He would never want to go back to the full-time staff of a college of education, though. 'One was split into so many parts.' He remembers how much he disliked the division between the academic courses, the professional courses, and the teaching practice; it made it impossible to have any continuity in relationship with the students. He also thought it wrong that all the lecturers in the academic subjects tended to come from grammar schools.

Looking back he is also glad that his days in the classroom, although they were pretty successful, are over. He complained about 'all the petty regulations which one is expected to enforce, and which enfold the teacher as well as the children'. Nor does he like the administrative tradition of dividing the day up into 35- or 40-minute sessions, and the demands of the time-table making arbitrary breaks in whatever one happens to be doing.

Now he feels the time has come to develop his own needs. If he was younger he thinks he would be writing himself; instead, as a small private publisher he gets his satisfaction from promoting the work of other people. Like Michael, he bothers about the split between the schools and the outside world, but views it from a somewhat different angle. He feels that it is wrong that so many of the good things that are started in school cannot flourish outside. He regrets that there is no way to go on with 'creative writing' as part of a civilised activity in the adult world.

Joanna is another person who feels that what goes on in schools and what goes on in the community at large are unnecessarily and harmfully separate. She sees the split in a different way from both Michael and John. What concerns her is that children have to live in two separate worlds of school and home.

To begin with, she was very keen to teach and, as her mother was a teacher, knew something of what she was letting herself in for. As a sixth-former politics and education were her main interests. She applied for a university place, with the intention of teaching after she had taken her degree. But that plan fell through when she failed her A-levels. So she did a year's unqualified teaching at a junior school—that was 'the year of intermission', when no students were coming out of the colleges of educaton because of the switch-over from the two- to three-year course and the schools were shorter-staffed than ever. She then re-took her A-levels, this time successfully, trained, did a good probationary year in a primary school, then one term with a group of 14- to 15-year-old educationally subnormal pupils attached to a secondary modern school. She then left the classroom to take up on a full-time basis what had for some time been engaging her leisure: organising and running informal play centres and adventure playgrounds. After three years she is now in charge of one, and, oddly enough, on local government rates her salary is higher than it would have been if she had stayed in teaching.

But that is not the main reason she stays out of the schools. She says the only thing that would ever persuade her back would be if she could have a little country school without time-tables or pressures from over-ambitious parents; but with family groups and parents allowed into the classroom. Her actual teaching experience was quite different. In the primary school where she taught, parents had to wait outside the school, they were not even allowed into the playground. This was only one symptom of the clash between her life as a teacher and the ideas she was working out in a community play centre.

Now that she has left the schools she may find she has a little more money, but she is also working far harder. Her time is based on a 38-hour week, but for two years she has consistently worked a lot longer than that. Her usual working day is from 10 a.m. to 9 p.m., and with two full-time and 10 part-time assistants she is responsible for the running of a play centre attended by upwards of 75 kids. And to make the worker harder for herself she insists on an almost completely unstructured set-up, as she feels that in this way the play centre has the most to give children of all ages, their parents and the community at large. And as for those long school holidays—she now gets three weeks.

She reckons she won't be able to stay the pace much longer—perhaps another couple of years. But she is convinced of the rightness of what she is doing. 'It's all so much more relevant to life than anything that happened in the schools.' So she persists in trying to make her philosophy live, confronting big problems daily. Does one tell the police if a kid does a job? She is not against authority—she has regular if informal discussions with a local comprehensive school about known truants—but as a serious citizen she doesn't always know where her loyalties lie; the forces of law and order, or the kids whose trust she's struggled for? When it all gets too much for her, what will she drop out to next? I asked her if she'd think of going into a more orthodox form of social work. She thought not.

Perhaps a person like Joanna must always be something of a lone pioneer. But would things have gone differently if she'd found herself in a more flexible school, more keenly aware of the links between parents and teachers, while she was doing her probationary year. It could be so—but of the friends she trained with only one is still teaching today.

There hasn't been quite such a heavy wastage among the set Sarah trained with, but it still is impressive enough. Out of a group of 12 friends only six are now still in the schools, and they finished their training only two years ago. Sarah herself left after her first term. It was partly a personality clash between herself and the headmaster of the school. But she was persistent enough, having made up her mind at the autumn half-term that she was going to leave, she forced herself to stay on till Christmas. And 'forced' is no exaggeration, for her unhappiness in school caused quite severe physical symptoms. She was literally sick every Sunday night at the thought of a new week. Her chief complaint was that the headmaster would give her no backing with her class, and every day she met problems of behaviour that she'd never encountered on teaching practice.

In fact her teaching practice was very successful, but ad- mittedly it was spent in fairly sheltered surroundings, with country children, who had neither the slick sophistication nor the sort of alienation problems of the children she was to encounter in her first post. Her first spell of teaching practice took place with a class of 14 eight to eleven-year-olds in a village school, her second with the third-year A stream in a small country town.

She was, in fact, trained at the same college as Mary, though, of course, many years later. Her mother had also done her training there. Her mother, she assured me, was a natural teacher and loved the work. She taught infants in the poorer parts of Birmingham during the 1930s.

But good teacher as she may have been, she didn't inspire her daughter with a burning desire to enter the profession. According to Sarah she just drifted in—or rather out of the four career alternatives offered to her in the sixth form it seemed the only possible one. The only other choices placed before her were to try for a university place or to become a secretary or a nurse. She now resents having gone straight from school to college to school again, and this may be one of the reasons why she decided to leave.

She married before she started work, so in her case it wasn't a matter of conflicting domestic duties. In fact, now that she works full-time in the production department of a publishing house, her hours of work are probably much longer, and her holidays certainly much less. It could be, of course, that later on when she has had some children of her own, as she hopes to, she will go back to teaching. Certainly she hasn't closed her mind to that idea. And that presents an interesting point. She will first have to do a satisfactory probationary year, before becoming a fully qualified teacher. Will she have to undergo yet another period of training before it, and if so what form will it take? The case is not unique. In 1968-9 (the last academic year for which figures are available) 3,701 young women non-graduate teachers under the age of 25 left the profession.

What lessons should we draw from these five random stories? They all seem to bear fairly heavily on two popularly mooted panaceas for the reform of teacher education: a more carefully structured probationary year and the broadening of colleges of education out from their present monotechnic set-up.

But would Sarah still be teaching today if more thought had been given to her during her first job? Certainly it seems that it might have helped her if her headmaster had taken a more positive responsibility for the probationers on his staff. But it wouldn't have helped her so much if she had been able to keep in touch with the college where she did her initial training, even had that been geographically possible, for she and her friends never did make any significant relationship with any of the staff. What John had to say about his feelings as a lecturer, on the effects of the atomised curriculum, might be relevant here.

Yet the theme that runs through all these stories is the more fundamental one of isolation. Why should all these teachers feel themselves, at all stages in their careers, so cut off from the community at large? Would it really end this isolation if the colleges were just to become training grounds for all manner of do-gooders from probation officers to teachers? It could be that such an arrangement would only harden the 'Them-Us' division: 'Them' who are trapped by the wicked ways of a commercial society, and 'Us' who try to save them from it. School, they say, is 'a preparation for life'. But actually there can be no such thing— one has to live as it happens, and teachers like everyone else want to do so fully.

In many schools we have liberated the teachers and the children out of the four walls of the classroom. Team teaching and the integrated day are beginning to put an end to that form of isolation. Perhaps the growth of the community school could do something to bring children, and teachers with them, back into the world.

9 Students talking about training

Richard Bourne

The view of both education students and probationary teachers about their initial training is essentially simple and essentially horrifying in its implications. Whereas the overwhelming majority of student teachers have deliberately chosen their course because they wish to teach, a healthy majority of them and of probationers are equally certain that they are inadequately prepared to do so.

In 1968 I asked a number of post-graduate students at the London Institute of Education to write me their impressions, related to their training, of their first half-term as teachers after they left the Institute. One of them, who has since become an active member of the National Union of Teachers, was a woman appointed to teach history in a large London comprehensive school.

She wrote: 'My reaction to my first half-term has been a mixed one. One of the factors which loomed largest during the first weeks of teaching has been that of discipline problems. With some classes I have met with much worse discipline problems than I had anticipated. A boy outrightly (and often accompanied by swearing) refusing to obey an instruction such as to move to another seat, or get out his book, is quite common. I have also had fights in the classroom, lighting up a cigarette in a lesson, football chants and stamping to drown my voice and a jam tart thrown at me when I attempted to remove it from a boy who was eating it in the lesson. Admittedly the most extreme cases such as the last one are rare, but the classes in which they occur are always difficult to handle. Many children in them make it quite clear that they have no intention of working.'

Simultaneously I had a letter from a man, who had trained as a science teacher, who had much enjoyed his first half-term at a London day public school but who was already saying: 'It is now my ambition to enter the field of education college lecturing, administration or even journalism.' His chief complaint about his postgraduate education course was that the science teaching method in which he was trained bore no relation to that approved in the school in which he did his teaching practice, and that whereas he was being prepared for grammar school teaching, his practice was in a comprehensive school.

'I found myself in a "new" (i.e. botched up) comprehensive school with some children who were definitely retarded and chaotic discipline', he wrote. 'It did not endear one to the comprehensive idealists. My tutor arrived at a typically noisy and disorganised lesson, watched the ensuing battle, and at the end said: "Well, I am sure I'd have done no better in this situation, I don't really know how to help you." '

Conversations with students and probationers since 1968, and a massive quantity of statistical evidence, show unwaveringly that not only in the problems of class management and curriculum studies but in other necessary attributes for a professional teacher, those who are now coming fresh to teaching feel unprepared.

A typically long and thorough 'interim report' from the London Institute of Education—itself a distillation of massive documentation from several working parties—covers the views of students in two bland paragraphs in its evidence to the James Committee.

'The students whose views we sought did not feel that they had had too much theory of education nor that too much time had been given to academic subjects. On the whole they thought the emphasis was about right. But the large majority think that too little emphasis is placed on curriculum studies and teaching methods, in short, on practical professional studies. The primary school teachers whose views we sought felt that they had been inadequately prepared in matters of class management and discipline, and they reported especial difficulties in administrative matters, in knowing how to form relations with the head teacher and other members of the staff, and in the teaching of reading.'

These laconic admissions conceal one of the most gigantic failures to reach an educational objective, as seen by those in the best position to observe it, that can be chalked up in the century of British state education. For this is not the failure of one area, or of one college, it is the failure of a whole machine throughout the country.

The National Union of Students conducted a national survey at the end of 1969 in which answers were obtained from 46 colleges and over 11,000 students. Of the total, 61 per cent of the men and 54·1 per cent of the women did not believe that their course would adequately equip them for teaching. In particular over 56 per cent of the total thought there should be more time spent on teaching practice, almost three-quarters thought that the lack of emphasis on professional development was the most serious deficiency in their course, and 87 per cent felt their college lecturers should be more in touch with classroom realities.

This picture can be filled out in more detail with the aid of other local surveys. Leicester education students, for example, tested opinion before submitting recommendations to their area training organisation. One of the most startling findings, after polling St Paul's College, the Domestic Science College, and the City of Leicester College, was that there was a favourable response, ranging from 61 per cent in St Paul's to 83 per cent at the City of Leicester, for the idea that students should spend a complete year's teaching before the third year of their course.

Overwhelming majorities at these three colleges felt that the need for compensatory education, particularly in educational priority areas, was not covered adequately, rather smaller majorities felt that they were not being sufficiently prepared for teaching in teams and across subject boundaries. In general, 63 per cent of the Leicester students felt that their education course work was unsatisfactory—73 per cent considered the history of education to be of little value—whereas large majorities thought it essential to be trained in improvising with inadequate equipment, in teaching mixed ability classes, and in relating to parents and social and psychiatric services.

A similar story comes across in one of the most statistically sound surveys of teachers in the first three years of their service— conducted by the Inner London Education Authority in a sample of over 1,000 schools in early 1971. Here, among teachers who had been trained all over the country, 82 per cent felt that too little emphasis had been placed on teaching methods in their initial training; 87 per cent had either received no specific training or were dissatisfied with the training they had had in helping emotionally disturbed children, 76 per cent responded similarly over the teaching of immigrants, and 69 per cent over their preparation for teaching slow learners. Further, 49 per cent reported that their training had not been very helpful in preparing them to maintain discipline and classroom control, while for a fifth the subject had never been covered in their training; 40 per cent or more stated that their training had not been very helpful with regard to class organisation or the use of modern resource materials of the Schools Council type, and as many as 45 per cent reported that there had been nothing about team teaching in their training.

The same survey showed that, whereas nearly three-quarters of the new teachers thought it desirable that a student should spend a full term at least on teaching practice, less than a third had done so themselves; and although fewer than one in a hundred thought teaching practice in one type of school was sufficient, a third of them in fact had had this experience in only one type. Over a half felt that on teaching practice they had been able to spend too short a time working with pupils outside the classroom or observing other teachers in the classroom.

Indirect but crucial evidence on the practical weaknesses of initial training came out when the same London sample was asked where the teachers recognised difficulties in their job: 79 per cent acknowledged some or much difficulty in dealing with individual problem children, and 77 per cent said the same about enabling children to work to capacity. In Inner London's educational priority areas as many as 26 per cent reported 'much

difficulty' in making contact with parents. An odd comment
on the way in which these new teachers were approaching their
task at a time of widespread educational and technical change was
that roughly a quarter felt that both developing innovations in
course content, and integrating the use of technical aids with
course content were not relevant to their job.

The significance of all this evidence of the failure of teacher
training as a vocational preparation is redoubled when it is
remembered that, far from the common assumption that all
student teachers are somehow refugees from other courses at
universities or polytechnics, they represent a high degree of
commitment to their vocation. The Inner London survey showed
that 86 per cent of recent teachers had intended this career on
entering higher education and only five per cent were frustrated
university applicants. Comparable figures in the N.U.S. survey
were 81·7 per cent and between 3·4 per cent and 18·3 per cent
(the question was capable of being misinterpreted), and in the
London Institute survey they were 81 per cent and 6 per cent.

However, although this shows a degree of solidarity with a
career choice which is probably quite as high as in other professions which start training their recruits at the age of 18, it would
almost certainly be a misleading picture of student attitudes if
taken in isolation. It would ignore three aspects in particular
at a time when the whole picture of higher education is changing.
It would ignore all the indications of dissatisfaction with the
certificate of education as a non-marketable qualification respec-
ted only by employers of teachers, a point which has been pressed
in comments by student officials on teacher education. It would
ignore also the rapid growth, backed up by demand from 18-year-
olds, in university degree, courses in which education is taken
alongside another subject and where no commitment to teaching
is assumed. And it would ignore also the significant evidence of
vocational dissatisfaction among B.Ed. degree holders.

Student dissatisfaction with the non-marketable certificate
qualification is a symbolic issue. It seems unreasonable to many
students, even if they have no intention of doing anything but
teaching, that they should spend three years in full-time post-

school education and not automatically be eligible for a degree at the end of them. (Even in the case of the existing four-year B.Ed., roughly half the men not taking B.Ed. and a quarter of the women would have liked to have taken this degree but were unable to do so according to the N.U.S. survey.) Putting it the other way round, many students consider that if the great majority of student teachers were working for degrees it would be far harder to explain away the poorer status and facilities that they perceive to exist in education colleges by comparison with the rest of higher education.

The sensational growth of degree courses in institutions outside the colleges, coupled with the declining applications for certificate courses in the colleges themselves, tell a supporting tale. For they strongly suggest that if there was no change in the colleges, and the universities and polytechnics were completely free to take as many education students as they liked, the certificate courses in the colleges would have to be wound up in a very few years.

But in view of the strong evidence that education students as a whole are concerned at the vocational inadequacy of their courses, and of the doubts that some express about the vocational content of the new mixed education degrees that are now appearing, it becomes important to explore the dissatisfactions of the B.Ed. students. For as things are now, with strong competition to get on B.Ed. courses among the ablest minority of college students, and with much criticism that in general the B.Ed. part of a four-year course stresses academic qualities to the exclusion of vocational ones, it is significant to find that the B.Ed. course can upset the vocational intentions of teachers.

The N.U.S. survey found that B.Ed. students were less likely to have entered a college because they wanted to teach, more likely to think that their courses failed to equip them to teach, more likely to wish that they had chosen something apart from teaching, and more likely to wish to be trained alongside other types of students. (Some of the details imply pretty clearly that the more competitive these 'brightest' college students perceived themselves to be in the general labour market, the less sure they were about going into teaching; for instance, the highest number of B.Ed. students wishing they were doing something else was among women training for secondary teaching, where almost a third had regrets; among the men B.Ed. students there was a sharp rise in those who would have preferred studying in multi-purpose institutions between those preparing for nursery, infant and junior work—36 per cent—and those preparing for secondary work, over 52 per cent.)

Although it is not easy to interpret the evidence conclusively it is also interesting that the I.L.E.A., in its survey of new recruits, discovered that the B.Ed. holders reported more difficulty than others in fifteen professional aspects of their work. 'In 11 of the 15 areas they reported "much difficulty" twice as frequently as all teachers taken together, and in a twelfth area they had the highest proportion reporting "much difficulty". Only in the area of administration duties did they report less difficulty than other teachers.'

The problem with a finding like this, of course, is that it could mean too many different things: it could mean that the B.Ed. holders were less well prepared for classroom realities by virtue of their longer, more academic training. It could also mean that the kind of temperament that is successful on a B.Ed. course is ill adapted to the gritty life of a teacher in school. It could mean, in correlation with the N.U.S. evidence, that people who were doubtful of their career choice and unpersuaded by the quality of vocational preparation are finding all their fears reinforced once they get into service; or it could mean, more optimistically, that critical intelligences let loose in the schools are more aware of problems and of the difficulties in solving them than uncritical or complacent colleagues.

But it is time now to turn to student attitudes to college and B.Ed. course work in itself. From the outset it must be made clear that student criticism of the familiar mixture of main subject, education course and the rest is certainly no sharper than that of contemporaries in universities or art colleges. Possibly, to the misfortune of the colleges of education, it has been less searching.

If one talks to a group of college students, however, one is likely to hear complaints and very probably conflicting complaints about the course content. There will be complaints from students who went to work in a primary school that the whole idea of having to do main subject English, for instance, is a diversion of their time. On the other hand, from someone who would have dearly loved to read an English literature course at a university, there is a complaint that the main subject is insufficiently rigorous and intellectually satisfying, or too circumscribed by the fact that its object is to produce teachers of English rather than just English graduates. More common perhaps, for a teacher who wants to work in a secondary school, is the complaint that although he or she may enjoy studying the Victorian and Romantic poets these are not the literary salesmen to have a knockout success in a downtown comprehensive school.

There are complaints that the main subject courses in the colleges are a pale reflection of what university departments were doing some years previously, complaints that the colleges, too, are merely elaborating the specialist subject straitjackets which students were pushed through in the sixth forms even at the very moment that some schools are trying to escape through integrated studies, multi-sided projects and the like. From this aspect, of course, the terrifying weakness of most colleges in the science, maths and technology areas means that few students can get an all-round education if they want one.

Some of the harshest words are thrown at the education departments and curriculum studies. Of the lecturers here it is often said by students that they are neither great teachers nor great discoverers of educational or pedagogic wisdom. It may be that the students are too willing to attack these lecturers here, and that the departments themselves have trouble in winning recognition in a quasi-academic atmosphere in which actual teaching prowess and curricular inventiveness are not universally esteemed. But it is a common grouse among students that the different doings of the education department are themselves scarcely integrated—that sociology and educational theory scarcely rub shoulders, let alone compare notes with the pedagogic methods.

And yet some students feel that they do not have enough time to come to terms with Piaget, or the underlying assumptions of the Plowden Report.

The education departments are bound to be a target of students who are not satisfied about the relevance of their courses. They appear to be poor relations in the colleges, yet they have to carry the whole burden of preparing students to be teachers at a time when the schools themselves are bursting out of the old academic assumptions. Sex education, teaching of reading, education for a multiracial community, participation in educational research and assessment of its results, team teaching, unstreaming and vertical family groups, community service and community schools, work experience programmes, the devising of C.S.E. exams within the school, oracy and an introduction to numbers for infants . . . the list catalogues an exploding universe of ideas, problems and changes which the education departments ought to be up with and stimulating their students about.

A number of students appreciate the difficulties. Some might argue that the non-education departments in the colleges ought to be hived off to universities or other institutions, to sink or swim there, leaving the education departments with the straight-forward job of teaching those who want to become teachers how to teach. Others might argue that the education departments themselves ought to be hived off to the schools, or federations of schools, to which students could then move for their vocational training.

One of the most popular developments among students, not only involving education lecturers, is the growth of team operations in which students and lecturers are able to do some teaching while the students themselves are actually learning alongside the children. The range of projects may run from combined work in playgroups or on projects in educational priority areas to the combined exploration of the social structure of a square mile of Notting Hill (undertaken by a group in their first year from the Digby Stuart College, Roehampton).

Although teacher unions are traditionally wary of unqualified teachers, even if they are students in training, it seems clear from

the experiments that have taken place that students can perform
a useful service—for instance, in motivating the slow learner or
supporting the poor reader who gets no backing in the home—
as well as learning about human development away from the
ritual confrontations with a class in teaching practice. Many
students in training have emphasised how much they have
valued the chance to get to know a handful of children really
well. With the emphasis in the schools switching to small groups
and individualised learning this is sound preparation also.

Though it is sometimes said that teachers are born and not
made, there is a strong feeling that the education courses could
do more to help students: they need their confidence raised by
seeing that they can help individuals and groups to learn, they
need to find that they can involve and stimulate the bored or
disruptive child, they have to discover how to be fair, how to
gain cooperation, how to keep their own tempers. But they
feel that they can only get this kind of professional competence
in a situation in which the colleges and schools have come
together. It cannot come about where they are shipped off to
schools, thrown into a sort of beargarden, and inspected at the
end of morning lessons for signs of a scratch. They need others
alongside them far more of the time.

Some of the students, though perhaps not enough, are critical
of the intellectual level of the colleges. They claim that there
are not enough books in the libraries, that the staff do not do
enough research, that the intellectual stimulus among the student
body is not engaging enough. But for every college lecturer of
whom a student can say: 'If you were any good you'd have a
chair at a university', the lecturer can equally turn round and say:
'But if you were any good, you wouldn't be here either'.

This is where both students and teachers are aware that the
education colleges are stigmatised in a socio-intellectual hierarchy,
quite irrelevant from the intellectual task involved in teaching
today. It is particularly ironic, as students themselves are the
first to notice, that at a time when the schools are moving to
mixed ability groupings and there is decreasing educational
faith in fixed intelligence or fixed intellectual rankings, the

colleges themselves are put in the situation of being eternal 11-plus failures in a caste system of higher education.

B.Ed. course work is liable to run into particular attack from college students, if only because it casts its shadow so widely yet so few are able to take the degree. Apart from the complaints about the variation in B.Ed. requirements from university to university, and the inconvenience involved in some colleges where a handful of students are on the course, the criticisms seem to be those of the certificate courses writ large. Either the courses are insufficiently vocational, or they don't go deeply enough into an area that happens to interest the student, or the contents are just old fashioned or uninspired.

One of the most interesting findings in student attitude surveys is the recognition of the importance of teaching practice, and the desire for more of it if possible. This is significant because many students are understandably apprehensive about it, and some have disappointing, miserable or embarrassing experiences of it. Student teachers suddenly placed in a class possess no automatic authority, and the children may just be trying to catch them out. In such a case the most carefully prepared lesson, most fluently given, can easily go astray. It is in such situations that students can feel themselves most helpless, or respond most bitterly: they may not be successful in handling their apparatus, they may have forgotten that children do not all concentrate equally all the time, and they may not appreciate that through no fault of their own they have inherited a class in which education is a state of total war, and nothing to do with collaborative learning.

It is in teaching practice that the student comes up against the reality of his prospective trade and needs to develop that strange mixture of technique, morality and good humour which is the hallmark of successful teachers. It is here that he finds that one child who is determined to tear a class apart can successfully prevent 30 others from learning anything for 10 minutes at a time; that he learns that if respect and initiative are lost in the first quarter of an hour they are unlikely to be regained for a whole period; that the objectives and values of many of the children coming to school, even in their most cooperative moments, may be totally different both from his own and those he is encouraged to impose on them.

It is when the student goes out into the schools that he becomes aware of conflicts between the pedagogic approach he has been taught in college and the style approved in the school itself. Given the total autonomy of both colleges and schools it is inevitable that there should be some conflict. But in fact the students on teaching practice may be surprised to find that the areas of conflict boil down loosely to a difference between modern discovery methods taught in college, and a desks-in-rows, reading primer approach in the schools.

After having slung his arrows at stick-in-the-mud colleges it may come as something of a shock to a student to find that they had been ahead of the schools, and this can set up lasting shockwaves. The I.L.E.A. survey reported that 50 per cent found a conflict in methods, and whereas 53 per cent said that this lay between informal college methods and formal methods expected in the school, only one per cent considered that it was the other way about; the second most highly rated area of conflict was 'streaming' versus 'non-streaming', and here again the colleges were the non-streamers.

The significance of this cultural divide between schools and colleges—which is primarily a product of their separation—can hardly be overstated where the students are concerned. On the one hand, it may make them doubt the reliability of the training they have received in the colleges. Can their lecturers actually practise what they preach, or are they only intellectually convinced of the approach they recommend? Why, if the approach is sound, have senior and experienced teachers still in the schools not seen the wisdom of adopting it? Of course, there are all sorts of explanations for the conflict. The older teachers have had poor opportunities for in-service courses to introduce them to different approaches, they may have had an inadequate initial education themselves, they may have been too busy keeping a school afloat through a heavy teacher turnover to have kept themselves as up-to-date as a good professional should, and they may just have got more set in their ways as they grew older.

But these other explanations are not always considered by the student teacher, who may instead accommodate to the *mores* of the hardbitten staffroom cynics, and reject the training received in college. Alternatively, of course, he may stick to the approach of the college and find himself in pitched battles with his old-fashioned head. On the whole such frictions seem to be greatest in junior schools and in the smaller secondary schools; but in the context of 'pupil power' movements among the teenagers and pressures for more participation in decision-making by younger staff, insecure and conservative heads can react in an ugly fashion if they perceive a threat in the student teachers and probationers.

In the circumstances, then, it is rather to the credit of students, and an indication of the seriousness with which they take their careers, that they tend to favour more time on teaching practice. For although no one can be sure exactly why people decide to leave teaching this conflict in outlook between the colleges and schools, with its resultant disillusionment and local friction, is probably one reason for the dropout among recently qualified teachers.

How do students rate the general social atmosphere of the education colleges? On the whole, compared with other areas in which the National Union of Students is interested, the colleges have been praised by students for their willingness to adopt participation in their government and academic planning. By all accounts this is frequently a more sincere operation than in universities, with a correspondingly high commitment by students to its effective operation. It is noteworthy that no education college has seen anything like the student unrest of some universities or art colleges.

On the other hand, students do not always accept the rosy view put about by college authorities that the colleges have outgrown the strict rules and rather limited horizons of their origins. The students still find that the tradition of the single-sex, church-financed, residential college dies hard in spite of superficial changes. They may still have to be in by certain hours and,

although the staff and governors may no longer be *in loco parentis,* they may still show a tender concern for their morals. The colleges have a much higher proportion of students over 22 than is normal in higher education, and they are unusual in that over two-thirds of the students are women. This sex ratio and its social consequences may help to explain why, in the N.U.S. 'attitudes' survey, a higher proportion of women than men said that they would prefer to be at an institution which included non-teaching courses. (Two of the most popular prescriptions for the colleges—that they should offer liberal arts courses or social service courses—might not significantly alter this sex ratio.)

Students at the colleges themselves are, of course, used to the imbalance of the sexes—though it may be that the proportions of men are building up in colleges which are developing large graduate certificate courses—but it is one big reason why students in universities and polytechnics would like to see the colleges integrated into their institutions. The feminine majority has often been quoted as the cause of a generally conservative and quiescent image for education students. But there can be a curious social flavour to an institution whose social tone is set by an Adonis of the physical education course, swooned over by admiring lovelies.

Although it is not true that the majority of colleges are set in the countryside, some students still comment on the romantic, anti-industrial attitudes which seem to pervade them. In this, the colleges merely reflect values which are more widely spread in the British education system and which may in fact be altering now. A hostile and suspicious attitude to the world of salesmanship and industry, a feeling that education must be puritanical, and a rejection of and ignorance about events outside the schools —these are sensed by some students, and irritate them. The students notice the way in which the colleges tend to look to the universities for approval, overlook what is happening in further education and nourish their own internal systems of snobbery.

So far we have looked at the views and feelings of students almost exclusively in regard to the colleges of education. Of

E

course, a significant minority of teachers come into the schools after getting a university or polytechnic degree and taking a one-year postgraduate certificate. It is here that some of the sharpest criticisms of teacher education are to be found for this one-year course commands the respect neither of the students, nor of the universities, nor of the schools.

Some students, who have enjoyed a pleasant three years at university, undoubtedly see in this course merely an opportunity to prolong their stay. By comparison with their three-year course, they often find it undemanding. But, though they have a degree and the Burnham financial increment that goes with one, they cannot pretend in the schools that they have picked up in one year the type of knowledge of children or educational theory that their contemporaries will have obtained over three years in a college.

This feeling of fraudulence, to which a number of postgraduates will confess, is supported by a realisation that the ideology of the single-subject teacher whose specialist knowledge excuses him his ignorance of child development, is fast being undercut by changes in the schools. Only a grasp of a range of subjects, and a solid knowledge of learning theory and class management, will be sufficient when nearly all schools are comprehensive, when nearly all groups contain a mixture of ability, and when most subject barriers have broken down. The very growth of three-year degrees including some education throughout is a hint that increasing numbers of students realise that the postgraduate certificate is an unsatisfactory compromise.

Finally one should emphasise that students generally, ably represented by the National Union of Students, are the one group which has seen most clearly that the existing hierarchy in higher education, a product of history and concern for prestige, is now a stumbling block both for the personal development of the students and for those professions, including school-teaching, into which they move. In this, organised students consider that they are in the vanguard of democracy: facilities should not be markedly different for people on different courses, and the best way to ensure fairness all round is by combining the different institutions at present into a comprehensive university or 'poly-versity'.

If the N.U.S. was to succeed in such a redistribution, the benefit to student teachers as individuals, and to education as a subject for intelligent attention, would be considerable. For it is an oddity, of which education students are specially aware, that they are expected to go out and maintain an education system which discriminated against them on grounds of academic and social prestige. They in their turn, as quasi-successes of the system, are required to pass on a set of values to large numbers of children who are not inclined to share them and who stand to get even less recognition by the education system than they have had.

One of the difficulties of student teachers in a permissive age is that they are the largest group of young people being prepared to intervene actively in the lives and attitudes of people even younger than themselves. Yet it is considerably more acceptable in contemporary ethics to pick a fight with a policeman than to pick a fight with a child. There is a trauma here for student teachers, linked to the fact that students are anti-authoritarian, and that teachers are traditionally authoritarian figures. But if student teachers, working for degrees like everyone else, were recognised as full partners in higher education, like everyone else, perhaps they could go out and play a non-authoritarian rôle with their younger brothers and sisters in the schools of the future?

But, for the present, student teachers reckon that they are not properly trained to teach, and that they don't get full value as students. And they hope Lord James is listening.

Part 3

Helping our teachers

10 Coping without the cane
John Ezard

'Mr Jones tried to throw me over his shoulder but I threw him over mine instead. As he hit the floor, I kicked his head hard. The other boys laughed.' (Comprehensive schoolboy, aged 15.)

* * *

'I know I shall never get promotion now. My troubles began when the assistant head called me to another classroom and said: "You're a big chap, there's something I want you to do." I found this 12-year-old—a nice kid but not very able—cowering up a chimney, tears and snot running down his face. Two masters wanted me to hold him across a desk while they thrashed him. I said: "If you touch that child I'll break every bone in your bodies." The staffroom didn't speak to me for a week afterwards.' (Secondary modern teacher, five years out of college, aged 31.)

* * *

'While London's new labour majority wants to do away with corporal punishment, the schools have become a battle-ground between the caners, the anti-caners and their pupils.' (*Sunday Times*, 1971.)

* * *

All these quotes reflect extreme and untypical situations. But there is a tension in English classrooms at present which too rarely surfaces into public discussion, partly because we are bad at organising the kind of inquiries which might detect it. A fair way to measure it is by talking privately about discipline to a largish sample of young career teachers, which is what I have done. So I pass on their conviction that much of this tension could be drained away by three reforms.

1. Stronger, continuously renewed injections of the experience of serving teachers into courses at colleges of education. The teacher-tutor system should be expanded on a basis of yearly or termly release from schools. Termly release would help a teacher to pass on really fresh experience to students.

2. A marked increase, as soon as possible, in the number of discipline discussion classes and simulation exercises held by the colleges.

3. Planned induction procedures for teachers of up to three years' experience starting at a new school. Staff operating this 'big brother' system should get responsibility allowances. This would, of course, take time and cost money. But the British Council provides the last two of these services for a few score lecturers it sends abroad each year to work with adults. Why can't we do it for those we expect to shape more than half the future? It's worth stressing that a class teacher with a high proportion of immigrants in Bradford can face a communication barrier appreciably worse than that of a lecturer in Baghdad, Manila or Delhi. Abroad, he can draw on a fading, but still predictable, tradition of reliance on English language and Victorian forms of behaviour. At home he is in a social melting pot.

When recent graduates talk about their problems of classroom order a common complaint is that 'I was pitchforked into it'. Of the 43 State teachers who have helped me with this chapter, *only three had experienced any direct discussion of discipline.* Only one had even heard of simulation classes, of the kind held by Berkshire College of Education, and that was at second-hand. This girl teacher, aged 29, said: 'The discussion at my college was, in retrospect, painfully inadequate. I can see their problem. Every authority and school has autonomy in techniques of control. So what's the point of trying to lay down rules which may be contradicted as soon as you go into a classroom? Oh yes, we had educational psychology lectures but, without experience, how could we evaluate them? I am having to learn everything from scratch and under pressure.'

A 22-year-old metallurgy teacher at a north-east London comprehensive said: 'The colleges are letting through far too many people who collapse as soon as they reach the classroom.'

Teachers would settle for induction over three years because they recognise that a longer period would require too many senior staff to spend too much time wet-nursing. It would also cover most of the early years in which a young teacher is moving between schools with contrasting regimes and conditions. Problems of adaptation have been multiplied since 1966 by the growth of comprehensives, which are mostly still fermenting institutions. In the livelier ones long-term relationships can be hard to forge. This is because pupils are being busily hived away into subject groups. Often worst off are the 'sink' schools, struggling with a high proportion of maladjusted children with criminal records against a background of parental violence, absenteeism, and varying degrees of racial tension.

The buck of the 1944 Education Act stops *here*. It is on these 'sink' schools that the rest of this chapter will concentrate: partly because the good comprehensives will, in the long run, probably work out their problems; but mainly because it is at such schools that an increasing number of college-leavers, faced with a constricting job market, are likely to spend their formative years, and go through their baptism of fire. At the end of the chapter are 10 rules-of-thumb for a teacher in a first class. They represent the hard-won lessons of interviewees who have mostly tried to avoid indiscriminate corporal punishment. A few of these were supporters of the Society of Teachers Opposed to Physical Punishment. Whether or not you agree with all S.T.O.P.P.'s viewpoints—and the group has achieved an influence in staff-rooms above and beyond its size or resources—you should find its preoccupation with discipline a useful irritant at the very least.

In general, the sample's experience implies that the median is not the 'blackboard jungle' school of popular folklore but the 'pressure cooker' class, where a multitude of inherently soluble small problems may build up into an explosion. In short, your kids are statistically *unlikely* to come at you with a knife, but they may use judo if you have been cursing each other for weeks. And while the phasing-out of corporal punishment does appear to be biting, as policy, it is also putting teachers at each others' throats.

To show this in action, I draw below on the stories of two young 'sink' teachers, Robert Andrews and Philip Hutchins, on the views of their two toughest pupils, on the comments of a psychologist, Dr Andrew Crowcroft, and on the ideas of Michael Duane, perhaps the country's leading anti-punishment theoretician. If you think their accounts untypical, remember Dr Crowcroft, consultant at the I.L.E.A.'s Woodberry Down child guidance clinic, North East London: 'Of the 150 schools I deal with, only 25 per cent have a healthy, creative atmosphere. Most of the others are *faute de mieux,* with hopeless problems. I find morale among teachers terribly bad.'

Names of teachers, boys and schools are disguised. If you wonder why, then your friendly neighbourhood education officer will be all too pleased to enlighten you. To talk identifiably about your school is, with too many authorities, to risk displeasure or even blight on the testimonial grapevine. (The National Association of Schoolmasters was justifiably angry about this grapevine at its last Easter conference.)

*　　　*　　　*

Until just three months ago, 'Jason' and 'Reggie' were Robert Andrews' hardest cases in his current maladjusted class in a South East London comprehensive of 1,100 children. At 15, both are impatiently pushing the school-leaving age-limit.

Jason is a fully-grown teenager, lithe and conscious of his Elvis Presley looks. He wants to be a sailor. When I said sailors have no regular sex life, he had already thought of it. 'Yes,' he replied, 'but I'm not going to drink. I'll save money and spend lots of months ashore between ships.' His reading age is seven, and he minds about it because he can't tell the time, and can't always hide it from adults like me. Reggie—fat, slow-moving and quick-witted—has already cast himself as the pilot fish to Jason's shark. Reggie supplies the words, facts and concepts that Jason gropes for. He rations Jason's 50p-a-week pocket money and tells him who to hit in the playground. His reading age is 12. He found out about this because his father refuses to take him into his lucrative Woolwich tobacconist's. Reggie can reel off tobacco prices like a veteran. But, rebuffed, he wants to be a docker. In that job he will need to find another Jason to survive. And, possibly, vice versa.

Jason: We're very lucky to have Andy. No one else ever took us out. He is the only teacher who does not beat us up. Brownie, he doesn't like talking in class or when you can't understand your work or if you can't draw something on the blackboard. He scrapes his hand down your head to your bottom. That squeezes your hair. Andy, he just takes everything as . . .
Reggie: A joke.
Jason: Yeh. He says things like 'Get off, you silly sod!' I once got hit off him when I kept shoving him.
Reggie: But you deserved that.
Jason: Yes. When he gets his temper up he is rough. But he takes most things as a joke. He is the only teacher who does not hit all the boys when one boy messes about. When you get hit for nothing, it just makes you want to hit back. You don't feel like work. I don't feel like working for the sods for days after. I had a fight with Brownie once. He said 'Start writing' and I got upset because you are not supposed to write in the book I was reading, it is for reading. I did not write and he kept hitting me round the head and shouting 'Start writing'. And I hit him back in his belly. It ended with him trying to throw me over his shoulder but I threw him over mine instead. As he hit the floor I kicked his head hard. The other boys laughed. I had to see Fat Arthur (the head), but all I got was a telling off.

Mr Govern is a rotten teacher, so we call him Hitler. He

only likes boys who are good at woodwork, and he hits you round the face with a bamboo if you are no good. Frankie Philips got stabbed outside his class once. Reggie, who stabbed Frankie?

Reggie: Neville James. . . .

*　　　*　　　*

Robert Andrews corroborates all these statements. Robert, 25, a Cambridge graduate only a year out of training college, says the key to Jason and Reggie was to realise they were 'like frustrated heroes of a novel by Alan Sillitoe'. Although attuned to casual violence, they had an embryonic sense of natural justice which could be stunted by thoughtlessness, or encouraged by a feeling of 'constructive relationship' with a teacher. His solution was to expect them to behave 'as nearly as possible like fairminded, normal people, while allowing generously for their failures to do so'.

He says, 'Jason still gets hit very savagely by the deputy head. With me, he kept trying to pick a fight, either to prove I was like the others, I suppose, or to show off his judo. It stopped when he hit me so hard in the chest that I lost my temper, cuffed him quickly and said, "Stop showing off and buggering everybody about." To my relief, he didn't come pounding back at me.

'In a sense my school used to be a Dotheboys Hall. One boy shot a teacher in the ear with an air gun. A girl teacher had a hand up her skirt. It leads to a "cuff the children down" attitude. There is a depressed staff-room atmosphere because, with all these disturbed children, they don't feel they are doing what they are trained for. Then in came a new head and felt the school was becoming just a caning machine. Only one boy has been caned according to the punishment book this term, but the head will not ban it because he does not want to divide the staff-room. A lot of the staff still hanker after the old system. I'm not being paranoid in saying that three-quarters wanted my class outings to fail. Every previous outing had been strictly policed, and they were afraid of my idea of letting the boys wander around freely, as a kind of lesson in coping with the world they will go into.

'But in this school you lose your links with boys like Jason and Reggie so quickly. In my class of 15-year-olds there was once an Indian boy who had a mania for collecting knives, and a mania for slashing other boys. Every morning I tried to search him. One morning he pushed me away with his hands and drew the knife. I just stood in front of him, called him by his Christian name and said, "Give me the knife. How would you like it if I attacked you with a knife?" He said, "Wouldn't mind, sir, wouldn't mind." I said, "But wouldn't you mind? Just think about it. It's wrong to cut people up."

'After a rather sweaty 15 seconds the brainstorm, or whatever it was, passed, and he gave the knife. The same boy once challenged my whole authority in the class. He pushed me quite savagely in the chest. I got him by the tie, threw him down on the floor and—I'm embarrassed to admit this—said: "Do you want punching?" Again the brainstorm passed, and he went back to his seat. We were beginning to get on, but he was moved to another class and he is still giving trouble. I wish I had him back.

'You can't be an absolute pacifist. You've got to be an empiricist. The important thing is to build a good basic relationship with each boy, call him by his Christian name, and make the classroom a pleasant place to come into. If they basically trust you the crises solve themselves. If you are a liberal I think you have a duty to uphold your values. It's an obvious truth, but it's worth remembering, that it can cost a liberal as much ulcerating effort to be violent as it can cost a fascist to be liberal. I believe education is a leading out, not a driving in. I did once have an elder brother come up to do me in. Another teacher managed to keep him talking while I sneaked out. It's very difficult to say, but if I got my teeth knocked out I would probably get out of the job.'

*　　　*　　　*

The description of confrontations between pupil and teacher could be of interest to every student who wonders how their three years of training can avoid giving them guidance on these matters.

In May 1968 Ivor Cook, the central figure in the Court Lees School affair, his wife, A. S. Neill and Michael Duane answered the question: 'How did you cope when you faced physical threats from children?' They gave their replies in *The Times Educational Supplement.*

Mrs Cook: Well, Neill here has allowed boys to kick him, haven't you? I think that's a marvellous thing to do.

Neill: I might not do it now!

Duane: I had a boy at Risinghill who wanted to throw a chair. So I said: 'Go straight ahead.' And he just put it down. When you face them with the possibility that they can carry it out, that they are not going to be stopped and bound and twisted and have their arms pulled, and all the rest of it, then they are defenceless. By showing that you are willing not to attack the other person you immediately put him in a defenceless position. He cannot go forward against you because you have in a sense capitulated.

Cook: I'll tell you what I used to do, and it worked. I don't say it *always* would. God knows what harm I did to them. If a kid threatened to hit me I'd fall, on my knees, sort of 'Spare me!', and so on, which was such an unusual thing for somebody to do that it did a number of things.

The class would roar with laughter, which was a bit disconcerting to the lad who was hoping to get backing, and it was a thing he'd never seen before. I don't know what would happen the second time! But it always worked the *first* time because it was something they'd never dreamt of happening.

*   *   *

Philip Hutchins is a wall of a man. Weighing 230 lb, he could lick Jason with one hand. Hutchins is an avowed non-corporal-punisher. This year, at 31, after five years at three 'dustbin schools' in North London, East London and Surrey, he is preparing to leave teaching.

'I get tremendous enjoyment out of children,' he says. 'I love kids, as my wife will bear out. But five years of teaching under these conditions have destroyed a great deal of the enjoyment. What really disturbs me is that it is not the children's fault. It is continually trying to succeed in a system which is basically violent, frustrating and repressive. The danger is that if it is going to take him six months to train a class to come in and sit down and work—train them by patiently putting up with the noise and quietly persuading them to do this—then he is not going to get this time. The teacher next to him will immediately say: "Look, we can't have this sort of thing."

'In my first class on my first day I announced: "There will be no corporal punishment during my lessons." Very soon this came to the ears of the second most senior teacher, a man who caned exclusively as a form of punishment. Then and there, in front of a great number of people in the staff-room, he said he would see I was out of the school. And he succeeded in this. He was afraid of the system which did not allow him to use the cane, not because he had a pathological desire to hurt people but because he was afraid of the children. But if you are an inadequate human being you are an inadequate teacher.

The worst caner I have ever come across was a man of 50. In my second school I saw him once hit a boy a dozen times hard round the face. He had told him to do something and he hit him until he submitted. Quite small boys were standing around him, and at least one of them was crying. The boy himself was *non compos mentis* for half an hour afterwards. He was quite incapable of speech.

'Nothing a child actually does is ever enough to justify the rage a teacher sometimes feels. Even with words you can destroy a child in front of his peers very early. Any teacher can do it. That is worse than corporal punishment. If a child is very disturbed from a very aggressive background I have discovered that the solution for me is to defuse the situation. Say something absolutely ridiculous like "Give us a kiss, darling" or "Don't get your knickers in a twist". My most successful gambit so far is borrowed from Dick Emery on the box. If a child really gets under my skin, I say, "Oh yew are awful, but I like yew." A lot of teacher's best punchlines come from television shows. You've got to keep in with their pop songs, their football and their TV viewing. If watching ITV on a night off bores you, too bad for you. It's essential homework.

'Of course, it wouldn't work for everyone. If it doesn't, and things are bad, you can withdraw yourself or make it plain they have hurt you. One of the most common insults in London schools is "You filthy Jew", and that really hits me where I live because I am a Jew. I had a child who was a real little racialist. One day it got too much. I said, "That's it, now you sit back and listen to me for 10 minutes!" For the next hour and a half I belted into them about what racialism had done to me and my friends. The boy still comes to see me, five years later, at home and he is a very different person.

'I find it possible myself to build up a normal relationship with kids, but only at the cost of destroying any normal relationships with my colleagues. The net result is that after five years I have one boy who comes back and sees me. Is the game really worth the candle?'

*   *   *

Dr Crowcroft is a grandfatherly chain-smoker who lives in a small Georgian house off Finchley Road. He was trained in a closed mental hospital. He left it in horror, knowing that he was deserting his patients but feeling that he could not survive there as a person. For the same reason, he advises Robert Andrews to quit his school as soon as possible.

This is how he sees him:

'He is a good, flexible, sensitive teacher. People who can bring gifts like his into teaching are the salt of the earth.

'But I wonder how long he can keep up his *élan vital*. I would predict he will find it very hard to stay for more than a few months to a year. You can't beat the ordinary, small, bad, political situation. In the long run I think the only situation is teacher power. I have been very struck in my experience as a school counsellor by the appalling standards of teachers as people and their incredible ignorance of their psychologies. It's no wonder you get these uncontrollable problems when you put children into large classes. We know what happens in animal populations when they become too crowded. We know sibling rivalry is at its height when too many animals of the same age are put together. Yet we are surprised if the point of no return is reached by the less stable individual child in this situation. It's precisely what you would predict in crowd behaviour after a football match. I would advise this man to move to a more tolerable situation. If the teacher turnover at his present school becomes too high, perhaps some lady councillor will wake up to the fact and do something.'

*   *   *

Michael Duane's name throbs through any discussion about classroom order. In summer 1962, as head of Risinghill Comprehensive, Islington, he told his school assembly he was abolishing corporal punishment at his staff's wish. At first the school was a chaos of smashed windows and sprung fire alarms. In 1965 the I.L.E.A. shut Risinghill—at a time when, Duane maintains, its disciplinary and academic record were coming to surpass those of any comparable neighbouring school. Of Robert Andrews, he said:

'Given time, I have no doubt the children will accept his pattern of relationships with them. But he is under tremendous pressures, from his fellow teachers and possibly from parents. At one point he says the children need to feel violent. I think they are simply searching for a pattern to which they have become accustomed.'

He also says that teachers must attempt to introduce a rational element. This is why the troubles at Risinghill went on so long—because at the heart of what we were doing was the middle-class conviction that you can socialise children through language. 'You can't do this if children keep being filtered out of your class. The children will quickly find out if you are a warm person who likes them. But good socialisation goes beyond that to the point when a child accepts you as he would a parent. They will test your reactions to the limit until they are satisfied you are the person for them.

'You must seek out the things that mostly interest them. You must give them plenty of opportunity to talk about themselves, their family and friends. With experience, you will at least identify their essential problems more deftly. But we must remember we are not plaster saints. We have to teach children that they can drive even a teacher beyond his or her personal limits. As Shaw said: "The only time to hit a child is in hot blood".'

*   *   *

GUIDELINES

1. Forget the cathartic 'To Sir, With Love' theory of getting on. You may make them love you one day but the next day they will shit on you. This is a fact of life, not a proof of failure. Nothing is permanent.

2. Avoid confrontations and radical changes of policy on impulse. If tempted, walk out and think it over. Cool it.

3. Be clear about your limits of honesty about your own life, and make these clear to children when they ask questions. Be consistent.

4. The ultimate violent situation can always be avoided if you insist your head of department or headmaster bears his full responsibility early enough. If you're afraid to call them in you can build up terrible problems.

5. In this situation don't be afraid of having the child moved to another class. If your class asks why, tell them.

6. Be clear about how liberal or authoritarian you want to be. Don't fluctuate too much. Your class needs a dependable pattern.

7. Before taking a job, ask the headmaster categorically whether

he allows corporal punishment—and check this discreetly with other staff. If still in doubt, ask to see the punishment book. Too many heads lie about it.

8. With a really troublesome child don't hesitate to share your burden by calling in guidance and welfare services.
9. But don't—very important—let them blind you with jargon.
10. Leave a school if you feel it is eroding your flexibility, because this is your crucial asset as a good teacher.

11 Children from another world

Eric Midwinter

A child in the corner is exhausted. His brutal father and feckless mother kept him awake with their fighting. This girl seems quiet. A few weeks ago she was terrorised by a teenage gang of extortion racketeers. This boy was scalded when his brother upset a kettle in the only room in his home. Twelve people sleep there. Those brothers are always by the window. They are called 'window-watchers' by the teachers. They live in a towering block of flats. This is the way they are used to seeing life.

These are children who attend an educational priority area school. It is the dark side of the teaching moon. It is the sort of school which is often forgotten by educationists and politicians. Touring students from most of the colleges of education rarely see such a school. They usually get taken to the open-plan, carpeted, blouse-and-tie-intake school on the other side of town. College authorities believe the 'pleasanter' schools are more in line with their teaching precepts. Most students coming to teach in E.P.A. schools will be having their first sight, TV documentaries apart, of the grim truth about teaching the disadvantaged in the decaying centre of the big cities. Dr Donald Lomax gave the clearest evidence of this when he interviewed 1,400 students. He found that *not one* had any experience of slum conditions. Such unlucky students are gravely handicapped when it comes to teaching in the toughest schools. '*Teaching* is perhaps the wrong word. The E.P.A. teacher is an educational Jack of all trades. Apart from the ordinary routines of any school, there are truants to be mopped up, injuries, sores and boils to be treated, adults to be advised on a range of topics from marital breakdown and housing to crime and punishment, emotional outbursts to be tended, family and other feuds to be quelled, and a host of other social disasters and miseries to be met. The E.P.A. teacher must be sleuth, nurse, solicitor, confidante, psychiatrist and pal all rolled into one, society's rep on the other side of the tracks, along with a clergyman here and a social worker there.' (The quotations on this page come from the pamphlet I wrote for the N.U.T.)

No one needs to be told that this kind of job specification is beyond the range of the most progressive, most aware brand of teacher education at present available in this country. Even the conventional educational terms lose their meaning when the teacher is faced with situations like this. In a down-and-out downtown classroom such pieces of jargon as 'low standards of attainment' obtrude almost as an afterthought.

Where do they live, these children with whom the first-year teacher, fresh from the sweetness of campus life (and, before that, most likely from an environment where, conventionally, one building contains one well-knit family), will be faced on her first working morning?

'Practically all of them will be living in sub-standard accommodation, denied even the basic civilised privacy of regular hot water, a bath and an indoor lavatory. Those who enjoy these relative luxuries will probably live perched sky-high on a towering precipice of flats. Which is preferable? Is it the tenement, seven or eight in a room, no doubt without gas or electricity (these having been cut off for non-payment), with drains blocked and fungus thriving on the inside walls? Or is it the flat, with human excrement in the lift, menaces on the stairways, drunks in the play area, frighteningly low walls on the balconies and a blockage in the refuse shaft?' Teachers living in areas such as Gateshead, Manchester, Birmingham, Cardiff, Glasgow or London often refuse to admit that the homes near *their* school are like these. It was amazing to read the letters sent to Leila Berg when the first of the 'Nippers' (Macmillan) books appeared. These were an attempt to get away from the vision of English life portrayed in *Janet and John*—that world of detached houses, ponies in the garden, and exquisitely behaved parents and children. Teachers objected to these 'low-life' stories. They said there might have been pupils from homes with outside toilets, leaking roofs, and low-income parents in the 1930s, but there was none now. One wrote: 'Everyone has middle-class standards today.'

Another teacher, from Essex, wrote: 'We realise not all children own ponies, etc., but neither do they live in houses with holes in the roof, have fathers who have to be pleaded with by their offspring to go to work. This is reminiscent of the "Victorian Melodrama" or "Band of Hope" literature'. This teacher then showed that he did recognise the realism of the stories by contradicting himself in this way: 'Surely it must be enough for them to *have* to drag Father out of bed before they go to school, without having to read about it when they get there.'

Some teachers even found the idea of a whole family eating fish and chips together quite incredible. It is difficult to begin to reply to such correspondents, but, as I write, I have just seen a news item, in a national paper, about a head who bought fish and chips for all his pupils (and a portion for himself) 'as a treat'. Such teachers as Mrs Berg's critics are so out of touch with the lives their pupils lead outside school that it affects their judgement of them and their parents.

Dr Elizabeth Goodacre, in her book *Teachers and their Pupils' Home Background* (National Foundation for Educational Research, 1968), disclosed how some teachers tend to generalise unfairly about the ability of the children in their care. She said: 'The teachers' lack of knowledge regarding the gradients of status in the manual classes was reflected in the tendency for teachers in lower working-class areas to see their classes as homogeneous groups, and pupils as predominantly children of fathers with manual occupations. Their tendency to stress the power and responsibility of occupations which in the past were related to educational mobility and hence intellectual capacity also led them to think of their pupils as intellectually homogeneous; more teachers in the lower working-class areas tended to accept that they had no pupils of above-average intellectual ability. Further, it appeared from their comments that their own language system and academically biased education might make it extremely difficult for many of them to recognise *unfamiliar* forms of intellectual functioning.'

Student teachers have to be made aware of these biases before they can cope with them. In more and more Colleges (for instance, in those that have supported the Liverpool E.P.A. project so staunchly) this awareness has been developed. But a much greater effort must be made in this direction. Unless students likely to face the dark side of the teaching moon are prepared, there is little they can do when they are confronted by it—except perhaps to resist the temptation to be shocked into complete withdrawal.

Shock, it has to be said, can be considerable. And shock, of course, must be expected even in schools on the sunnier side of town. Indiscipline, along with bullying and other school vices, is by no means exclusive to educational priority areas. But colleges need to face students with the truth that teaching *anywhere* is not an easy job, that it can be testing to the character, threatening to the person and wearying to the spirit; and then to add that the tests and threats and weariness are greater in E.P.A.s than elsewhere. It is certainly reasonable to ask why this student was not better prepared, since the particular school must have been on the college's regular teaching practice roster and some news of its nature must have filtered back to college over the years.

The fact is that teachers taking up posts in E.P.A.s are moving into a cultural and social context with which, unless they are positively instructed about it and exposed to it, they can have nothing in common. This comes to the surface in a number of ways. Take values like thrift. Teachers have been drumming home the virtue of thrift for a hundred years. But to be thrifty in city areas is to be 'a mean bastard who won't stand his corner'. Or take language. As Bernstein has pointed out, the teacher's not understanding the child is as effective a communications block as the child's not understanding the teacher. One sometimes sees a child, on some trivial issue, driven into a block of this kind from which he feels forced to escape through 'impertinence' or worse.

Add to cultural differences of this sort, based on working-class or ethnic origins, the historical shortcomings of the education system and the fact that we now retain young people in school under substantially the same Victorian regimen as children of five; and you need hardly be surprised that new teachers get the catcalls and the jam-jars if they come into the schools apparently (and usually in fact) with every intention of supporting the *status quo*.

There are, however, teachers who are eminently successful in teaching the socially disadvantaged. They may not be the sort of teachers who are recommended in colleges as stars of the observed lesson, but they make E.P.A. classes *work,* and that's what matters. Without doubt, one secret they will have discovered is that 'You can't win 'em all'. Given the context of social deprivation from which the children come to school for a brief period—six hours out of twenty-four, remember—it is no use pretending that everyone will become adjusted to the alien system and benefit from it. There are lordlings of misrule who should perhaps be paid a handsome retainer to stay away from school. We have one education system, and millions of children. It would be foolish to claim that at present it caters validly for all of them. Teachers should not expect too much from their efforts.

What, then, *should* teachers do in response to the problem? The successful ones have done two things. Some have found for certain pupils a place in the élite; as an ex-working-class head wryly remarked, the only answer he could offer was reading. The teacher, as likely as not an able ex-member of the skilled working class, is usually well prepared to deal with the exceptionally able child, whether in an E.P.A. school or elsewhere. He knows the ropes; why, he used them himself. But although there is still a pool of academic potential to be realised in priority areas this is not the major problem. The major problem is the majority—the thousands for whom there is no place in the élite.

Other teachers, especially at the primary level, have tried to help children to enjoy school, as a counter to the grimness around them. This is admirable when it is done with sympathy and without condescension. It is an approach which recognises that education is not necessarily preparation for the future but that it is for the here and now; an approach to which children respond enthusiastically.

Both these approaches have their obverse sides, and too often the line is crossed by the insensitive teacher. A rigorous approach may produce short-term control and favourable C.S.E. results—and, one must confess, a certain satisfaction among teachers. But it is wrong in principle and practice. It is intolerable that a school should be based on the rule of fear, and it stores up trouble for the future when the child moves into society and the sanctions are removed.

One must not, mind you, be mealy-mouthed about corporal punishment, when the system protects the child pretty effectively. But where is the protection against the mental cruelty which one occasionally finds, and which is invariably worse? One has seen the sullen child, of six or sixteen, beaten down by nagging. Most children would settle for a belt across the knuckles with the board-duster and forget about it. There is also the question of self-defence. Twice in socially disadvantaged schools I have been attacked by big boys. It was probably my fault for provoking them, but I didn't hesitate to defend myself physically. There is no time, on these occasions, to conduct a rational argument with your better nature.

The children come in 30s, not in ones. If 29 are doing fine, and *one* is disturbing the class, have you the right to spend hours with the oddball to the detriment of your work with the other 29? It's a dilemma. A clip on his ear may give the 29 a proper chance; it may also cause the singleton to become a manic depressive shoe-fetishist. As an 'educationist', you mustn't do it. As a teacher, you may have to. Perhaps corporal punishment should be abolished but not done away with.

Now for the other approach, the child enrichment one, and *its* darker side. Some teachers, with the best of intentions, have tried to make the school a cultural shelter where the child is protected for a few hours from the social blitzkrieg. Within the class, all is sweetness and light. The trouble is that, unhappily, the blitz lasts for 24 hours a day, and not just for the six hours that children are in school.

Both approaches—whips and scorpions, or sweetness and light —have a common outcome: boredom. Progressive methods help, but more valuable are sympathetic teachers and a relevant curriculum. What is required, above all, is an intimate knowledge of the area, its people and its children. The teacher must understand the values, the argot—in short, the social context of his pupils. This must inform his choice of aims and methods, and these will vary enormously from one area to another.

A sound classroom approach, a pleasing school climate and relevant teacher education are all clearly possible. These elements work together in the urban community school, where one can see a stable partnership developing between school and home, and between school and community. The teachers know the parents and involve them in their work. At the same time, the school ventures out into the district. Students on attachment to the school join in this corporate life and learn at first hand of the difficulties they will later face.

Such a school would naturally adjust its curriculum to more 'social' and less 'academic' purposes. While promoting traditional attainments, it would equip children to view their social setting critically and to respond creatively and positively to its problems.

Not enough schools do this; not enough colleges are producing teachers equipped to man such schools. There is a confrontation of attitudes here. In the schools, teachers tell students, in a favourite phrase, to forget the 'airy-fairy nonsense' they learned at college, to get their feet on the floor, and to start knocking some sense into the kids. Back at college, tutors are telling students to ignore all the cynicism they will be exposed to in the school staff-room and to concentrate on individual nurture and bags of creativity. It's hard to decide which group is the more tragic: the staff-room neo-realists, advocating dreary and unreal teaching, or the college idealists, full of educational piety and impossible dreams.

Students, probationers and young teachers are all caught up in this contest. The first point they must realise—certainly in E.P.A.s—is that it is a *non*-contest. Many of the quarrels about formal and informal methods, or discipline and freedom, are falsely based. If the teaching content is irrelevant, it doesn't make much difference whether the children are sitting in serried ranks or swinging from the gas-lamps. Aim and content come before method, and too many teachers have allowed methods to become ends.

There are two questions which teachers should ask themselves apropos each piece of work. First, is it relevant to the immediate experience of the children? Second, will it contribute, in some way, to their social development, bearing in mind the likelihood that many of them will live out their lives in run-down or redevelopment areas?

The next step is to enlist the assistance of the home. The lesson to be learned from middle-class areas is that the school is the home *in extenso*; that the school in the socially deprived area must be made viable *for its area*. A socially relevant curriculum is a step in this direction, and, to date, the most successful child-parent projects have been based on local environment studies. In other words, parents are more likely to commit themselves if they feel that the material is both useful to their children and comprehensible to them personally. Since the Plowden Report, and especially since the inauguration of the national E.P.A. projects, it has become clear that education is a saleable commodity, as long as the resources are available. The myth of the feckless working class has been nailed. Parents in disadvantaged areas are, normally, alive to the difficulties of their children and vitally concerned for their future. They reveal a respect for the schools and an appreciation of the teachers' professional skill which does both sides great credit.

What is needed to spark off this potential is sheer know-how. E.P.A. parents are, almost by definition, school failures who didn't do well at school themselves. Even within the terms of what they know of the system, they failed. Seeing the mysteries of i.t.a., Dienes apparatus, creativity, discovery and experience, they wonder how on earth they can help. There are, of course, difficult parents, just as there are apathetic teachers; but generally E.P.A. parents are splendid people, anxious to join in if only they are shown how.

So it is an important part of the teacher's job to help the parents, partly by reordering the curriculum so that it has a 'community' orientation, partly by developing the school as a social centre, and partly by publicising its aims and methods. Well-presented exhibitions; publications; displays at focal points such as shops, factories or clubs; 'live' demonstrations of children's work; social/educational visits by parents to school, or teachers to homes —all these are ways of achieving this. The finest are those whichengage the parents on the shop floor of education, where they can see the process at work and, by involvement, understand it.

Above all, it is important that teachers and parents come together easily to discuss a child's schooling. Too often, teacher and parent meet in some eyeball-to-eyeball confrontation. This is not necessarily a matter of parent-teacher associations, with fund-raising dances; nor is it parent-power; nor is it teachers' aides, with all the attendant fears of professional dilution. It is essentially to do with seeing the parent in a learner rôle, with the teacher educating parents to help their own children.

There are no easy solutions to the problems of parent-teacher understanding. Some say that teachers should live in the area so that the commitment is complete, but *contrived* residence could be harmful if it appeared patronising. The Plowden Report emphasised the value of home visits, but before embarking on these one must be sure that the opening doors will reveal a welcome. Each teacher must perseveringly work out independent answers to this crucial question of home-school relations, for answers *must be found*.

Colleges have, in the past, paid too little attention to parents. Many is the time that Plowden is quoted in lecture-rooms— but rarely the passage to which I have just referred. Too often it has been possible for the student to emerge from his three-year course without ever having heard the word 'parent' uttered. As a result, generations of teachers lack the training to handle this most tricky of professional skills.

Even when teachers admit the need for home-school links, they are often genuinely worried by the thought of obstreperous mothers or power-mad fathers; these are proper fears, and must not be dismissed out of hand. But in E.P.A. schools teachers may console themselves with the realisation that parents are even more bothered than teachers about possible intrusions into the others' domain. Only time will bring a feeling of familiarity, with teachers and parents accepting their new rôles.

I do not, believe me, minimise the practical obstacles. Teaching in educational priority areas is not for everyone. There is, *of course,* an urgent need for a new type of teacher who will take up this challenge, which is conceivably one of the few hopes we have of avoiding social disaster. An élite is needed—and quickly; and this élite may well need special salary increments, top-class staff accommodation, first-rate technical, welfare and clerical services, low teaching ratios, and so on. But these are decisions for the authorities. In the meantime, young teachers of the socially disadvantaged must rely on themselves.

One aspect of the whole problem particularly concerns the younger teachers and the students—the difficulties involved in teaching certain immigrant pupils. Students tend to *overestimate* the need for special training. It is unlikely that the vast majority will ever be called on to communicate with non-English-speaking coloured immigrants. Even though 76 (out of 146) local authority areas in England have substantial numbers of immigrant children in some of their schools there is no need for *all* students to have special training. It is best in most cases to think of underprivileged immigrant pupils in the same way as other deprived children. Their problems still stem from poverty, bad housing and inarticulate parents.

But those students who are going to teach in Bradford, Brixton, Birmingham or Brent should be given special help. Government aid is needed to provide enough centres in such key areas to give all young teachers an in-service course from experts, running concurrently with their job. Once again, as we have seen elsewhere in this book, the dilemma arises from the shortage of good, veteran teachers. Should they be in the centres, teaching the teachers, or in the schools with the children? It will be a long time before we have enough good teachers to staff the schools *and* the centres.

Although most students will benefit more from worrying about how to cope with behaviour problems or an alien working class culture, there are two points about immigrants they should bear in mind. They arise directly from the immense study of the coloured school population by Bert Townsend of the N.F.E.R.: *Immigrant Pupils in England* (1971). He found that 43,000 of the 262,000 immigrant children have severe language difficulties. These difficulties were enough to make them incapable of following the normal school curriculum. He also found that the authorities were concentrating almost exclusively on English for children from non-English-speaking countries such as India, Pakistan and Cyprus. Little help is being given to West Indian children speaking Creole or some variant of local 'English'. As there are 109,000 West Indian children, the largest immigrant group, this finding should be considered by anyone making decisions about the training of teachers.

Two other points came out of Mr Townsend's research, which will give the young teacher some idea of the complexity of the mine-field. Immigrants in general, and Asian pupils in particular, were often much keener to be educated beyond the leaving age than the local white working class. As a result, in some secondary modern schools with 45 per cent immigrants, about 75 per cent of the fifth-formers were immigrants. Young teachers should beware of assuming that *all* parents in E.P.A.-type areas are unenthusiastic about education. As we have said, it is necessary to nail the lie about all poor parents being 'feckless'. It is also essential to recognise how the different immigrant parents can have totally different attitudes towards the value of schooling.

Mr Townsend also demonstrated how unfair it is to give

immigrant pupils some IQ tests. His examples will show the need for careful choice of words when dealing with a multicultural class. Pupils reacted differently when asked to spot the 'odd man out' of (1) Airplane, Gas, Diesel, Automobile, Train and Bicycle, and (2) Grapefruit, Ortanique, Guava, Tangerine, Ugly. He explained that in the first example the English child usually said bicycle—as it has nothing to do with engines. A child from Barbados finds the test difficult because there are no railway trains in his country. The Jamaican pupil calls a railway train a 'diesel'. In his second example immigrant children were much better acquainted with the fruit than English pupils. Few children know that an ugly is a cross between a grapefruit and an orange. Few know that a guava is not a citrus fruit. Fewer still know that an ortanique is a type of orange.

Mr Townsend also made the point that English children are surrounded by squares, rectangles, and circles (paving stones, bus-stop signs, etc.), but the child from a rural Asian village is less used to these symbols which are such a vital part of IQ tests. This kind of information is useful background. It is also helpful to realise that one Asian child can have more in common with an African-born pupil than with another Asian. The biggest mistake is to assume that all coloured children have similar problems.

These points illustrate a tiny part of the problem. But patience, experience and expert help are the only long-term assets in the struggle.

There are no 'tips for teachers' with the socially disadvantaged. There are no easy solutions. But the finest single encouragement is the hundreds of teachers who manage it brilliantly. And it is not too pious to say that the non-material rewards and challenges can be commensurate with the fatigue and disappointments. At the same time, for colleges whose students have an even chance of working in such a school, it is little short of dereliction of duty to ignore the fact that these schools exist—and exist not as curiosities but as the living representation of education in many areas of our large cities. At this moment, the career for which colleges are preparing a significant proportion of their students will be begun (and may even be entirely conducted) in gaunt buildings isolated by demolition schemes, in overcrowded classrooms where the children are resentful, the paintwork peeling, the staff facilities minimal, the demands almost overwhelming. At least, we should tell student teachers the truth.

12 The teaching of reading

Ronald Deadman

It is time someone stepped in with a white flag. The war between educationists who seek to raise the status of the teachers by force-feeding their intellects, and those who prefer an approach geared to severely practical skills, must stop. Plato versus the Dinner Register never was a fight worth watching—and it never will be.

I believe that we shall solve the problem by linking what is academically respectable to what is psychologically and morally satisfying. And what better stimulus could there be than showing would-be teachers that 'social malnutrition' exists in Britain and offering them a prescription for its cure?

Right at the start of their college term (better still, in their sixth forms), students should be told that, in spite of massive university expansion, the child of a manual worker stands only one chance in a hundred of getting to university. They should be told, too, that there is now enough evidence to suggest that the obstacles are not as insurmountable as was once thought; that far from being a fixed, innate quality, intelligence can be developed, *and that the best tool for doing the job is language.*

It will be argued that lecturers in education are already communicating ideas like these. It is true, of course, that ongoing work in the sociology and philosophy of education includes Basil Bernstein's theory of elaborated and restricted codes. It is true, too, that the colleges spend a great deal of time impressing upon their students the need to examine the links between home and school. In spite of all this, precious little productivity—in the

F

form of higher achievement on the part of children from poorer areas—is apparent.

One reason may be that teaching in colleges of education is carried out in watertight compartments. What point is there in directing the student's attention to the lack of concept-forming language in the homes of manual workers if one hour later we shall be directing his attention to the nuances in Miss Jane Austen? Is it not possible to find better links between reality and literature?

So far as the reality is concerned, we can point to examples which many students will already have met in their secondary schools, if only at a distance. What, we might ask, has happened to the pupils who spent their time struggling with material which could have been written in Martian for all the effect it had on them? And since many of these pupils will now be getting married and producing children, will the wheel of educational failure *ever* be broken? We can point to a girl like Linda, who will now be working in the local Marks and Spencers. Books are not going to figure prominently in her life or her husband's. Linda can read, of course, and the *Sun, TV Times* and *News of the World* will meet her limited needs. She might even pick up a paperback by Barbara Cartland while her old man has his nose buried in *Shoot* or *Titbits,* or when there's nothing on the telly but discussion programmes. Never let it be said that we didn't educate the working class to a certain standard at least: they are, after all, consumers.

The idea of exchanging real language with her child instead of television folk idiom will be foreign to Linda. 'Leave off!' 'You must be joking!' 'Do you mind?' will spring readily to her tongue, and her husband will note, in moments of anger, that someone has taken 'a diabolical liberty'. Who will explain to them both the barriers set up by their use of the spoken word?

Who but the teacher of the future, who has been trained not to compartmentalise knowledge but to find the thread which binds it all together? For this task he will need an entirely fresh approach to 'literature', using authors like Wesker, for instance. Who can better link Bernstein with the painful facts of experience?

Beatie, a Norfolk girl (in *Roots*), is talking about Ronnie
Kahn, the young Jewish intellectual whose ideas she has tried
desperately to absorb:
'Once I was between jobs and I didn't think to ask for my
unemployment benefit. He told me to. But when I asked they
told me I was short on stamps and so I wasn't entitled to benefit.
I didn't know what to say but he did. He went up and argued for
me—he's just like his mother, she argues with everyone—and I
got it. I didn't know how to talk see, it was all foreign to me.
Think of it! An English girl born and bred and I couldn't talk
the language, except for to buy food and clothes. And so sometimes when he were in a black mood he'd start on me. "What
can you talk of?" he'd ask. "Go on, pick a subject. Talk. Use
the language. Do you know what language is?"
'Well, I'd never thought of it before—hev you?—it's automatic to you, isn't it?—like walking.
' "Well, language is words" he'd say, as though he were telling
me a secret. "It's bridges so you can get safely from one place to
another. And the more bridges you know about the more places
you can see! And do you know what happens when you can
see a place but you don't know where the bridge is?" '
Some will find no fault with the rôle Ronnie Kahn plays in the
life of Beatie—is he not, after all, attempting to cross the gulf
which exists between his own culture and hers? But objections
will at once be raised by progressive educationists who hold
the view that education for the working classes can never succeed
while the teachers remain simply reflections of the middle-class
ethos.
The best spelling-out of this heart-searching problem can be
found in Michael Duane's chapter in *Children's Rights**. 'From
Bernstein's analysis of the effects of the restricted and the elaborated codes on the outlook and capabilities of their speakers,' says
Duane, 'it is clear that a large proportion of the disciplinary
conflicts that arise in schools, and particularly in schools with a
large number of working class children, arise from the clash
between the teacher's middle class cultural expectations and those
* Elek Books.

of his lower working class pupils, each failing to understand the point of view of the other and each disvaluing what the other holds dear. The teacher sees himself as a missionary whose task is to reject the child's culture, language and modes of perception and replace them with his own.'

No one in his right senses is going to accuse Duane of not having the severely deprived child's interests at heart. But (and this is what must be resolved if teachers are to achieve the correct balance between heart and head) in the long run perhaps missionaries are really the only people who can at one and the same time be totally sympathetic to the deprived child's plight and totally committed to the idea that education can lift him out of it.

Bernstein himself has this to say in *Education for Democracy*:* 'We should start, knowing that the social experience the child already possesses is valid and significant, and that this social experience should be reflected back to him as being valid and significant. It can only be reflected back to him if it is part of the texture of the learning experience we create.'

Well, of course, yes. Who will disagree, except the most unrepentant Black Paper writers? But the questions we should put to Bernstein are these. Is there not a danger that some teachers will not allow the situation to develop beyond the social experience which is valid and significant at that time? Shouldn't teachers, at an appropriate moment in the child's day, perhaps when approval has just been given for a job well done, suggest that another mirror exists—one in which he may perceive a chance of escape from the educational priority area he's in at the moment? If this is paternalistic, isn't it more paternalistic to assume that the child isn't capable of being extended academically?

The response from colleges of education to Duane's belief that clashes take place because of the teacher's 'middle class cultural expectations' should be: 'Very well: what can we do about it?'

To start with, lecturers in English should realise that the cultural expectations Duane refers to have developed in learning situations, and are capable of change through learning situations. The literature syllabus is in their hands. They could open up new

* Penguin Education Special.

worlds—in terms of sociology as well as art—if they provided a reading list which included Wesker, Sillitoe, Storey, James Baldwin, Sid Chaplin, Waterhouse, Lawrence and Naughton (and perhaps Behan) and excluded Miss Austen, who has enjoyed a good run in the students' sixth forms, anyway.

Lecturers who are in touch with what the best primary schools are doing will know, of course, that the literary revolution has already begun. They will know that intelligent teachers are rejecting material which alienates the working-class pupil and are turning to supplementary readers like Leila Berg's *Nippers*—which get down to the nitty-gritty of the experience the majority of their children have to live through.

Gone are the stories of indulgent uncles buying ponies for Cynthia to ride into first place at the gymkhana. Instead, teachers, as well as children, now grin hugely at characters who (horror!) eat fish and chips in bed. And lecturers who keep up with what is happening down at infant level will also have noted Brenda Thompson's onslaught* on 'the banal, self-satisfied and basically unscientific' Janet and John books, and the 'unbelievably bad illustrations and archaic text' of the *Happy Venture* series.

But we are talking of books used by children who can already read. What about the thousands who haven't mastered the skill before leaving the infants—those who will become, through sheer frustration, grim statistics in the progressive divergence scales?

In a sensible world, we would agree that since restricted-code-using girls in the secondary school are very shortly going to marry and produce restricted-code-speaking children, it might be time we stopped keeping our 'middle-class' knowledge to ourselves so selfishly and handed a little of it on to the people who need it most. Ideally—and this is by no means a Utopian notion, since several secondary schools have already adopted such a measure, by linking community service to the curriculum— girls of fourteen and fifteen should be allowed to run playgroups in school time, organising painting sessions in the school grounds and learning how to cope with the young child's urgent needs in language.

* *Learning to Read* (Sidgwick and Jackson).

This, of course, is precisely what should be done in colleges. Playgroups and nursery schools—in which, it should be stressed, both men and women students would work, probably on a rota system—would at one and the same time provide the practical base for all the theoretical work being done in pre-reading skills and redress the balance between the middle-class mothers in the area who can afford to pay for such a vital service and the working-class mothers who can't.

As for reading itself, the time has surely come to step back and ask ourselves a number of extremely embarrassing questions. Since so many people are aware of the fact that children who are two years behind in reading at the age of eight may remain two years behind for the rest of their school lives or even get progressively worse, why are the colleges generally failing to improve the situation? (There are notable exceptions; Edge Hill College, Ormskirk, for example) Why are primary school heads in London complaining that too little emphasis is being put on the teaching of reading at college?

Let us listen to an imaginary lecturer in education at an equally imaginary college in Loamshire.

*　　　*　　　*

'I have called this meeting' (he will begin) 'to tell you that in spite of all the lectures in reading you will be attending in the next few years, and in spite of all the essays you will be asked to write, half of you, at least, will complain bitterly during your probationary year that you have been given no tuition in the subject whatsoever.

'The truth of the matter is that it is just not possible to teach people how to teach reading. However, for the next three years we shall proceed on the assumption that it is. Since it is part of our job here at college to stretch you intellectually, we shall do our best to make academically respectable what the average middle-class mother takes in her stride between cups of instant coffee, and without any training at all.

'Ideally, of course, we should bring into college children in need of remedial help from the local schools, supplying both the children and the students with that one-to-one relationship the middle-class mother enjoys. Instead, we shall do our best to achieve it with the help of books, resigned to the fact that the 35-to-1 pupil-teacher ratio you will enjoy in your probationary year will make a nonsense of our teaching, no matter how talented you are.

'We assume that, either during your probationary year or very soon afterwards, you will stop actually trying to teach reading and start talking about it instead—in seminars, on refresher courses and at the annual conference of the United Kingdom Reading Association. This is where we can help you. A brief glance at the chapter headings in the books we shall supply will convince you that the subject is just as satisfying intellectually to adults as it is in practical terms for children. One of our most popular books includes a chapter on "Processing the perceptual output". I'm sure you'll find it fun. Another will assure you that teaching children to read English by concentrating on the whole word is to ignore the fact that the English language is an alphabetic language and to attempt to teach it by whole words is to treat it like a non-alphabetic language such as Chinese.

'You may, however, find to your cost that the various combinations involved in systematic phonic training are comparable with Chinese as well. It's a funny old world we live in, and no mistake. We'll take three years to teach you all we have been told to teach you about reading, while the average middle-class mother will be doing it in three months with the help of a Ladybird book based on the key-words reading scheme (12½p).

'You can read. The child can't. You have to make the sympathetic leap into his world, with everything conspiring against you—an overcrowded curriculum, a tyranical timetable or a too generously integrated day. The chances are that you will receive far too few opportunities to help only one child at a time. You will become frustrated. You will stop doing what is vital to the process—explaining the most difficult words on the page before the child gets to them, so that there are no hurdles in his way, so that he can win your approval for mastering yet another portion of his book. You will instead become irritable and join your colleagues in the staff-room in a chat about reading ages, backwardness, the need for more remedial help in the school and (more likely than not) the dripping tap in the classroom which is driving you to distraction.

'But I said the problem was not insoluble. Research into the effectiveness of the initial teaching alphabet can't possibly show one of the key factors which helped towards its success: the fact that the teachers had, as it were, started all over again themselves and were learning it—enjoying it—with the children.

'And that, probably, is what you must induce in yourselves— an almost fanatical zeal which will communicate itself to the children you teach. It is possible that some of you find it necessary to consider reading not as an isolated skill, crucial though it is to the development of mankind (*pace* Mr McLuhan) but as part of a programme called *language arts* or *communications*.

'Whatever you decide to do, you will fail dismally unless you yourself are as highly motivated as the children you are working with.'

*   *   *

Is our lecturer's parting thought about language arts a trifle too optimistic? Few teachers in their first year are given the opportunity to re-jig the curriculum, after all. Most are forced to follow in the tracks left by their predecessors. This, however, is no excuse for the college not inducing the sort of unrest the subject of reading deserves.

John Sceats, a principal lecturer in education at Balls Park College of Education, believes that the phrase 'teaching reading' implies a narrow and inadequate approach to the whole question, and that 'making children literate' is a better description of what we should be doing. In such a programme, he says, reading would take its place as one of the components, and writing as another—the two being closely related.

He is, of course, correct in pointing out that everything we read is 'writing'. What we have to teach is written language, of which reading is the receiving aspect and writing the transmitting. Sceats compares two methods which a child might use to learn a word. One way is just to look at it and try to remember it. The other is for the child to say it to himself as he writes it down. The second method, clearly, is the better—because the child is more actively engaged.

Writing, says Sceats, is more closely related to reading than is often supposed. Written language can have the same power as spoken language, for words that young children *know* become their property—they delight in using them as tools for sending messages. As a most useful extension of what Sceats says about the power of the written word, students will find parts of Bruce Kemble's book *Give Your Child a Chance** valuable—particularly the chapter dealing with the captions parents can put under their children's drawings, and the concertina booklets they can make— all containing pictures of items which 'make the same sound'.

Young teachers would be wise to give a great deal of import- ance to writing, anyway, whether it played an important part in the reading process or not. We can be fairly certain that much of the frustration shown by children in twilight areas can be traced back to the difficulties first encountered in the highly complex task of translating the spoken word into a written form. Vygotsky, the Russian psychologist, tells us that, compared with the ease with which they can communicate in other forms, *all* children are seven years retarded the moment they pick up their pens. Subtract from this the two years compensatory experience some middle-class children will have enjoyed in nursery schools, and you will see why nagging about spelling and handwriting can drive the deprived child into a shell—worse still, out of it, into a position in which he can communicate only through vio- lence.

From the very first stages, therefore, teachers will help the child translate *his* spoken language into *our* written form. Here we must remember Duane's words earlier in this chapter. If the child informs us that the picture he has drawn is of his cat Toby and tells us that his dad says 'Toby is the greatest' or 'Toby

* W. H. Allen.

G

is smashing', then those are the words we encourage him to write (or write *for* him). There is no earthly reason why teachers should not write their own comments underneath the same picture as well—as part of what will appear to be a game to the child but which in fact will stretch him linguistically as well. This does *not* mean he 'corrects' the language the child has used in the first place.

What we are aiming for in a programme in which speaking, writing and reading are interwoven is the point at which the child will be able to demonstrate what Robert Ardrey calls 'ultimate identity of the first order.' Reading isn't necessarily a passive activity, and as John Sceats says, children should talk about what they have read, say which stories they liked best, and why. They can re-tell stories and improve on them, provide illustrations, invent questions to ask the next person who reads the book and so on. But the sense of identity they must be encouraged to bring to the surface will develop only through art and writing.

So far as writing is concerned, we shall be very lucky indeed if we can get work from our children like this example from the Daily Mirror anthology, *Children as Writers*.

Me

When anyone asked me to write a story or a poem or a play I always sit for such a long time thinking what to write about and in the end, if it's at school I get into trouble because I left it so long I don't write anything and if I do write I spell it all wrong and get into trouble for that, so it's just as bad any way.

I've been kept behind at school today because I do not attend to my teacher during lessons. He told me I must write two hundred lines of three words. Look Listen and Learn. It's on the blackboard so I can spell it right. Look Listen and Learn Look Listen and Learn Look Listen and Learn Look Listen and Learn. I'm fed up. Each time my teacher said Look Listen and Learn he hit me on the head with his knuckles. That is to make it sink in. If I looked and listened all day and night I would not learn because I am a dope.

I start off listening because my teacher has a loud voice and you can't help listening to it and if he thinks I'm not listening he bangs on his desk and makes me jump and I look because sometimes his false teeth drop down a bit on some words and he makes a little slurruppy sound when he catches them up with his tongue. I long for them to fall right out on to his desk and sometimes he thinks I am interested in the lesson because I look for ages to see them drop out but he always manages to catch them up in time. He's got hairs sticking out of his ears and when he scratches his chin they waggle in and out. I am the awfulest boy in the world because I would much rather look at his teeth drop and his hairs waggle than look at the blackboard.   David Dekon, aged 11

Few lecturers and students will quarrel with the judges who found a place in the anthology for David Dekon's slice of experience. Yet will they be able to say clearly why they enjoyed it? If they can, if they can cut through some of the mystique which surrounds 'creative writing' in the primary school they will be doing a job that needs doing urgently. Too often, students take with them to their first school ideas about the subject which add up merely to half-digested intellectualisations. No one has explained to them that writing like David Dekon's succeeds because it leaves no gap between the experience and the re-telling of it; they will cheerfully accept 'creative writing' of a different nature—a string of words like *rumbling rippling tossing* and *tumbling* which is intended as poetry, or a hotch-potch of longer words which prove that the writer has at least a gift for what has been called 'recollected literariness'.

Charles Causley is the man to explain what a poem does to you. 'Ten minutes after you've read it,' he says, 'you should feel as if you've been hit over the head with a sledgehammer.' Students should be hitting their lecturers over the head with sledgehammers themselves—in the sense that Causley means it, anyway. They should be given far more of a chance than they are getting at the moment to produce creative writing of their own. In too many colleges, writing is looked upon by students simply as a penance: lecturers in subjects like physical education, for instance—a subject which surely cannot be pinned down on paper—make the students write essays in time which should be used for writing poems and short stories. (As an example, the writer, during a brief spell in a college of education, was told by a gifted student that she wouldn't be able to complete her short story that week: she had to write a thousand words on the Duke of Edinburgh's award scheme.)

As for speech—the third vital factor in a language arts programme—lecturers would fail in their duty if they did not stress that its function is not simply a matter of establishing a social bond between the youngsters who use it; it also provides the most valuable opportunity possible for deprived children to absorb some of the concept-forming language the more fortunate pupils in their unstreamed class will be using. This said, students may also need reminding that the spoken word has its limitations. Given a tape recorder, and an imaginative teacher, younger children will make enthusiastic progress in reading, by relating sounds to symbols. Older children, given the same resources, will enjoy conducting interviews or producing their own lively versions of radio dramas—complete with sound effects. But it would be a great pity if, with time, enthusiasm for *spoken* English robbed us of future poets and novelists. In terms of art, it could be asserted that nothing worth saying can ever be entirely *said* (except perhaps on the psychiatrist's couch). Jack Beckett, a secondary schoolteacher, whose work with slower learners is reproduced in *The Keen Edge,* encouraged one youngster to produce this piece of verse:

> 'My mother's love went agine
> When she married agine
> But I found a greater love with my step-brother,
> And in my pale Harry
> A love that will never die.'

Could this have been done in a lesson devoted to spoken English?

There are, of course, many books which deal with that aspect of communication we call speech. Hundreds of them. Most miss the point: English goes far beyond the tip of the tongue; All are based on something called 'oracy' and all are incomprehensible enough to make the reader wonder why God gave man the power of speech in the first place.

13 The teaching of numeracy

Gordon Pemberton

What *is* the educational value of asking a child to divide 5 yards, 2 feet, 9½ inches by 7? This kind of thing can be found on blackboards, in textbooks, and in examination papers. It could appear in many children's work schedules and few parents would question it, for they had to do such 'sums' at school themselves. Few teachers would bother to challenge the educational value of such work, and many might even express the view that sums of this kind had always been done.

But the answer is quite clear. There is *no educational value whatever* in doing this kind of calculation. Such a calculation is a wicked waste of a child's school time. If it is supposed to be good practice in calculation, even better practice would be a similar calculation in different number bases, though those are done in real life by ready-reckoners or on simple calculation machines. If it is supposed to be a practical problem in measurement then we must ask: 'For what practical purpose does anyone need to do this calculation?' The truth is that this calculation, like many of its kind, is pure arithmetical rubbish. How, then, did such rubbish ever get into the school curriculum?

We must go back 100 years to find the explanation. The Education Act of 1870 made schooling compulsory, and the first job was a physical one—to round up the children, and get them into school, often in the face of violent opposition from parents who were losing the income from their offspring's child labour. Having got them all into school and locked the door, the next problem was to decide what to teach them. And it was here that the ambitious middle-class parents took over (and have held on for a century). 'Make good clerks of them!' was the cry. For in those days the clerkship was the coveted position. It meant clean, regular work, some security and social status. So the three R's were the first things taught—Reading, Writing and Reckoning.

When they came to arithmetic, they gave the children the kind of things the clerks did—addition, subtraction, multiplication and division, called the 'four rules'. There was no provision for those who were *not* going to be clerks—potential miners, weavers, builders, seamen, railwaymen and the like. *All* children were taught on the assumption that *some* of them would make good clerks.

Soon it was realised that they would need to calculate costs if they were going to be clerks, so the word went round, 'Teach them the four rules in money'. Later it was found that clerks had to deal with quantities and measurements in their costings. 'Right—teach them the four rules in yards, feet and inches, in gallons, quarts and pints, in stones, pounds and ounces.' The easy habit grew until the whole fundamental of school arithmetic was based upon the four rules in everything. Percentages? Proportion? Decimals? Vulgar Fractions? You name it, they did it.

After the examination system started in 1902, and was blown up to gigantic proportions by the 1944 Act, teachers began to teach children specifically for the tests and examinations. These were set by people brought up on the 'four rules', which gave further emphasis to the 'clerical' arithmetic.

Such is the tightness of the grip that the four rules have had on early public education that 100 years later they are still with us, and in great strength. 'They must know their tables and their sums' is a cry that will receive loud approbation at any teachers' meeting. So the professional answer to the question asked earlier is: 'We do sums of this kind because we have always done them.' And teachers who go so far as to ask: 'Why do we teach this kind of out-of-date arithmetic?' are immediately labelled as fanatics, extremists and faddists.

Who is to blame for the fact that many young teachers in many schools are being obliged to teach arithmetic of a kind that they know to be largely useless? Who is to blame for the fact that the vicious circle cannot be broken? The blame lies in most directions. It lies in those primary schools which pay more heed to their pupils' chances of selection for grammar school than to their understanding of the fundamentals of number. It lies with those publishing houses who know what they ought to produce, but issue the old stuff because it sells better. It lies with the producers of standardised tests in arithmetic. A large amount of blame lies with the grammar schools for their keeping their pupils' noses down to the examination grindstone and confining them to what can be done at the blackboard or in the exercise book.

But by far the greatest blame lies in the colleges of education and the departments of education of the universities. It is here that the vicious circle could be broken, but isn't. It is here that students could be shown the mathematics that children should be learning, but aren't. The college should be the place of re-appraisal, of getting down to fundamentals, of asking whys and hows, of critical re-examination of the content of education. But nothing of this kind happens. Mind you, there are extenuating circumstances. All but a few students come to college from grammar schools and they are used to two things: remembering and conforming. These youngsters have just finished a seven-year sentence of being told what to do and doing it. Any mental initiative, or reasoning power, they may possess indicates latent abilities undamaged by their grammar school, rather than fostered by it.

Thus the college tutor is faced with an expert in remembering and regurgitating. But the modern teacher does not need talents of this kind. In fact, they comprise the very antithesis of teacher training in a modern society. The student needs to be able to think and reason, to compare and discriminate. He needs to be able to tackle his own ferreting-out of information, and to make his own judgements in the first place. He needs to *challenge* the principles upon which modern education is based. He needs to look at the content of education, and pick out the dead wood. He needs to speculate in general terms on methods of learning— how did he acquire his own skills and experience? To put it briefly, he needs a questioning attitude towards his work, *the one thing he hasn't got!*

When a medical student begins his training he is shown right away the basic principles of what his future job is all about— the bits and pieces of people which go wrong. The only thing that is known with any certainty about a college of education student is that he wishes to teach. And so the obvious thing would be to put him into contact right away with the first principles of his future job.

But what happens to him on arrival at college? Is he soaked, or even dipped, in the atmosphere of education? No, the first few weeks of his new life consist of a cattle market of subject options and combinations. He will do 'main' this, and 'subsidiary' that, and 'professional' what-have-you. He has a time-tabled course, half lectures and half writing. In fact he continues with the same old grind, a chalk-and-talk syllabus. He listens, he takes notes, he reads and produces essays, living a life almost the same as the one he has just left in the secondary school. Some of the subjects may be different—education, psychology and sociology —but the routine is the same: read, remember and regurgitate, the student's three R's.

On top of this, we have a situation where students are trained to teach in primary schools by a majority of people who have never themselves done so, or whose efforts have not been fruitful. This would not be so disastrous in a static situation such as we had a couple of decades ago. Doing what was done before is slightly better than doing nothing. But education in general, and numeracy in particular, are not in a static situation; they have undergone fundamental changes, and the situation is now that education is on a newly based philosophy.

It happens that some of the most far-reaching changes in the curriculum have taken place in mathematics. These changes have not crept in; they have been shouted from the roof-tops for all to hear. The published material on this subject is vast, and so are the educational aids produced in connection with it. It is featured in television documentaries, and the national popular daily papers. And though it is by no means universal in schools, its impact has been felt far outside the teaching profession. The corollary to this is that all those who have anything to do with the training of teachers should be familiar with the changes themselves, and with the newer materials that are needed for learning them.

Would that this were so! But it is not. Many of the students coming into schools on teaching practice, or as probationer teachers, have not much idea of the first principles in the learning of number (simple arithmetic), nor have they much idea of how to organise the work of a class along these lines. Most of them have been trained in the idea that children achieve numeracy best on a class basis (all the class doing the same thing at the same time), out of a textbook, and with the teacher from time to time demonstrating at the blackboard. Among the staffs of mathematics departments are some honourable exceptions, all of them doing good practical work in difficult circumstances. But their efforts are merely scratching the surface. Most progressive schools have to assume that the students know very little about modern developments in the teaching of mathematics.

Colleges seem to have difficulty in deciding which department should be responsible for mathematics method, particularly for students who are intending to teach in primary schools. Is it the maths department or the education department? The level of difficulty of most primary maths is fairly low, if you are considering mathematics as an academic discipline. Even with modern primary maths, the conceptual and calculation levels are those of learners, and young learners at that. Thus such work is far below the students' level and far below the level of the work for which the lecturer was awarded his degree. So heads of departments and lecturers disdain this work. There are two things they should do. First, they should show their students—*all* students going into primary schools, not just those taking maths—the modern content of primary maths. Secondly, they should show them how to manage the learning situations of the children who will be in their classes. But what are their real attitudes? How do heads of college departments view these responsibilities? I discern five types—in ascending order.

First there is the tin god. He is usually a highly qualified mathematician and well advanced in his career. He allows no interference in the academic side of his work and is interested in the exam results of his students rather than their showing as potential teachers. He is full of prejudices, and this is reflected by the books and apparatus that are *not* in his departmental collection. One of these, a lady in this case, said to me of a well-known piece of primary maths apparatus, 'I wouldn't even have it on the premises!' Yet she knew that more than a dozen schools in the locality were using it and that her students would practise in these schools.

Next comes the *laissez-faire* type, usually highly qualified, amiable and very unsure of himself. There is very little co-ordination in his department, and he allows his lecturers complete freedom in the hope that the general effect will be successful. He does very little that is positive, so that in some cases groups of students have to *ask* him to deal with particular aspects of the subject. When challenged for his own views he uses such phrases as, 'It is not for me to dictate . . .' and he is unwilling to give any kind of lead in any direction. He is not insincere or indifferent, he is just incompetent.

Third is Mr Do-It-Yourself, superficially very confident and assertive. In his department there are all the books, apparatus, gadgetry and gimmickry that you could wish for. He makes his views loud and clear to every visitor, 'I like my students to get to grips with these things themselves. We can't possibly cover all the methods of all the schools, so we provide all the materials we can and then it's up to the students to make detailed studies of their own.' He calls in primary heads to talk to his students and eulogises them as 'experts' who have 'wonderful schools'. Though he may do his academic work well, he does little else, for the bare fact is that, as far as primary content and method are concerned, he can't do-it-himself!

Fourth is the Nuffield neophyte—harmless but not very helpful.

This type is sincere and enthusiastic to do his best for his students, but he lacks experience of primary schools. He tends to be establishment-minded, and so he quickly latches on to the guides of the Nuffield Maths Project, which he begins to use as a kind of bible—a substitute for first-hand knowledge. His argument usually is that if he gives his students 'content and method' according to Nuffield he is doing exactly what is best for them. But his lack of experience of primary schools prevents his realising three things. The Nuffield Guides, excellent as they are, provide for the extension of a school's own work; they are not courses. Many schools are not doing the kind of work suggested in the Nuffield Guides, though their work is of high standard in 'progressive' terms. Finally, a significant number of schools are openly antagonistic to the Nuffield type of mathematics. Thus the students from these colleges can become quickly disillusioned and bewildered.

Finally, we have the realist. He's usually been a teacher, often in a deprived area. He's interested, to a point of fascination, in how children learn and he tries his level best to enthuse his students along these lines. He organises as many school visits as he can, and he fetches in teachers of all persuasions to talk in seminars. He promotes discussion and argument about every aspect of school work—content, method, apparatus, gadgets, gimmicks. He is always provoking his students to ask how and why, and is never satisfied with his own efforts. If you ask him about his work he will probably say something monumentally modest like, 'We don't know the answers, but we try to make sure that our students understand what the problems are'. I take off my hat to these men and women, of whom I know several. Their students go out into the schools prepared to find anything from class table-chanting to wholly integrated individual work, and able to cope with either. But they are small in number.

What about the education department? They are not in the least like the other departments. In some ways it can be said that they are neither fish, flesh, fowl, nor good red herring. When the subject departments say, from their lofty disciplines, that it is not their job to show the students how to teach at the low primary level, the education department replies, with some justification, that it cannot show the students how to teach everything. Most education departments take the view that their job is to deal with such things as educational history, educational systems, educational principles, educational psychology—the theoretical side of the job. (And it is at this stage in the discussion that the teachers in the schools are entitled to ask: 'Who in the hell at the colleges shows the students how to manage a class of kids?') But the theory dealt with by the departments of education does not always ring true. What kind of theory are they putting over?

For instance, the current view of education is that it should be child-centred. We should help a child to learn as much for himself as he can, and let him go at a speed of which he is capable. As far as numeracy is concerned this means experiments and assignments on an individual basis in classes of wide ranges of ability. For diversity of ability doesn't matter in a class where children are doing most of their work individually, though such diversity has sociological advantages.

The student, on teaching practice in such a school, is expected to come to terms with a roomful of children carrying out simultaneously as many as a couple of dozen different assignments from the simple to the complicated. He has to be able to help those who are in need of it, and this means that his mind, and his concentration, will have to switch rapidly from one topic to another. He will have to deal with grammes and graphs, with sums and surveying, with pence and pendulums, all in the space of a few minutes. On the other hand, he must learn the importance of not interfering when children are making good progress; in fact, to leave well alone.

But hundreds of students I have spoken to in many parts of England are at first bewildered by these 'child-centred' methods, and the integrated work which flows from them. The students seem to have had no warning at all of these methods, and no preparation in how to cope with them. Moreover, their tutors seem to be put out, rather than pleased, by the situation. Tutors have to assess the *teaching ability* of their students—and how can you assess the teaching ability of someone who is not actively teaching, in the chalk-and-blackboard sense? How can you assess someone who is moving about the room dealing with the needs of individual children? How can you observe his techniques of questioning, and listen to his vocabulary level? How can you detect the strength of his preparation or his rapport with the children? The answer is that you can't do any of these things in a classroom where individual activities are taking place. But the education department of the colleges have not yet realised this, and have not yet done anything about it.

Students are still expected by their tutors to 'teach' in the traditional sense (even though this makes utter nonsense in a class of children of mixed abilities). A common remark of tutors, when they open the classroom door and find the student supervising the class in individual activities is: 'I'll come back when you're teaching.' Education departments must be indicted, along with the others, in that they don't practice what they preach. Popping into the classroom for half an hour, once or twice a week, never had very much meaning in terms of assessing a student's potentialities. Now it has no meaning at all. A student's grasp of child-centred and integrated work, his ability to adapt to a supervisory rôle, and his success at managing this kind of work, can be judged only by continuous observation of his efforts over several weeks. The teaching practice system, as it applies to modern methods, and in particular to numeracy, is a waste of time.

What is the problem in its simplest terms? It is this. We have to take young men and women from secondary schools at the age of about eighteen. We have to continue their academic studies, in some cases to a high level. We have to give them a good deal of the theoretical side of educational principles and child psychology, for they need an underlying philosophy for their work. We have also to expose them to children and schools, and let them practice their future job under supervision and guidance. And it would be no bad thing to put them for the greater part of their course in a building where they will mix with all kinds of other students (of all ages) who are pursuing similar courses of study, but for other jobs.

Let's sort out the staff first. The academic subjects can be handled wholly by academics. They'll like that, especially if their department is given university status. The theoretical side of education can be left to a mixture of university-style lecturers and practising teachers. The latter can be teachers seconded by their L.E.A.s for their expertise in particular aspects of the curriculum or in classroom organisation, management. They should be seconded for one year only, for fear they are brainwashed by the academics. But all supervision of students in schools must be done by *practising teachers and nobody else*.

Let's take the case of typical aspiring teachers, just finished their seven-year secondary school sentence. Their first year—yes, the *whole* of it—must be spent (a) mostly in schools of the age level in which they intend to work and (b) partly in schools of other age groups. During this year they will be supervised in two ways. In the L.E.A. in which they are working there will be a couple of general supervisors (man and woman) who will first place them in schools, and then visit them occasionally to see to their social and professional welfare. These supervisors will have the authority to move students if there are good reasons for doing so. The student will also be supervised by the head or senior teacher in the school itself.

What will they be doing during this year? Let there be no mistake about what I mean. They will be pupil teachers, learner teachers, apprentice teachers, call them what you like, but they will be dogsbodies, sharpeners of pencils and guillotiners of paper until they and their supervisors agree that they should have a try at the real job in a small way. But the main point here is that they will, over a year, absorb classroom atmosphere, organisation, and management and will learn a good deal of what the job is about. It is worth noting that the best 'class teachers' of the past century were undoubtedly those who were first 'pupil teachers'. My bet is that an initial classroom apprenticeship along modern lines will produce the best providers of learning for the next generation of children.

Their year away from academic studies will do them no harm, and when, in their second year of training, they attend lectures on the theoretical aspects of education, they are all the more likely to extract the full meaning from these. During their second and third years of training they should do a total of at least one term's teaching practice. And this 'official' practice should, again, be taken right out of the hands of the colleges, and put into the hands of the schools. Thus the grand total of one year and one term in the schools, out of a training of three years, is about the right proportion.

A degree? By all means, but let this be a general degree such as B.A. or B.Sc.—the indication of one or two subjects taken to a slightly higher level. But let's have none of this B.Ed. nonsense at the training stage. Of course we want a graduate profession ultimately, but to dub a student Bachelor of Education before he even enters the classroom as a teacher is ludicrous. Anyone who wants a degree *in education* should first do several years' teaching and be adjudged a *proven* practitioner before being admitted to such a course. At this moment I know several B.Ed.s and at least one M.Ed. who can't teach. The fact that they are all college lecturers, and don't have to teach, makes no difference at all. Allowing people to gain degrees in education by mere academic study is the debasement of what could be a valuable qualification.

In all the arguments about teacher training, however, the one thing we must not lose sight of is the simple fact that we want to train teachers to educate children. And this is not a complicated matter if we look at other professions. Whilst it is natural that the academic and professional sides of the job should be done by highly qualified academics and professionals, it has to be pointed out that good doctors are made in hospitals, good lawyers in courts and good captains on ships. Good mathematics teachers can be made only in schools!

14 In-service training

Michael Pollard

It comes as a surprise to recall that only in the past decade has it become accepted that a teacher's formal training does not end with his departure from a college of education.

Certainly, while teachers of my generation—I was trained in the mid-1950s—left college realising that they would discover during the next few years in the classroom the truth about teaching, they did not expect to need further training in methodology. At some time in the future, after five years' teaching service, one could try to get on to one of the extra-year specialist courses taken on full-salary secondment, but for this privilege many might call but few were chosen.

These courses apart, there were 'refreshers' of every variety—evening, weekend or holiday—but these were generally held to be for older teachers, or for those who wanted to notch up evidence of professional keenness to show on their application forms for promotion. The average youngish teacher did not reckon to need retraining, and although he might sign up for the odd course he did not, I think, do so out of a sense of professional need.

Often, refresher courses fulfilled a rôle in the pattern of teachers' social lives. Teachers would sign up for a course of evening instruction in, say, educational mime much as other people might enrol at the evening institute for basketwork. Apart from the negative pressure exerted by *Details of courses attended* on application forms, there was no sense of obligation to attend; nor was there any suggestion that regular course attenders might be better teachers than those who had other, non-professional ways of occupying their time.

Few teachers in those days were aware that the reign of the four rules in arithmetic (and, indeed, of the term *arithmetic* itself in respectable primary school usage) was drawing to a close. Few teachers of reading could know that Janet and John were threatened by revolutionary forces at the palace gates. Few teachers of secondary school science were conscious that the law of demonstration was about to be replaced by the law of discovery. The curriculum was still a fixture about which a consensus of educational opinion existed. The winds of change might be at work in Africa, but they were not yet blowing through the schools.

Nowhere, perhaps, is the generation gap among teachers so marked as in their attitudes to in-service training. I suspect that even now teachers of, say, 35-plus tend to regard it as a necessary evil—one of the penalties of teaching, like the slow grind up the Burnham Scale or the smell of wet raincoats—while their younger colleagues accept it as a symptom of change in the education system. I have noticed that the more stirring calls for a better in-service training programme have come from such groups as the students of the London Institute of Education, the Young Teacher wing of the National Union of Teachers, and so on. Whether this indicates that their college training has failed to give young teachers the professional security they need, or suggests that they show more professional responsibility, is a matter for conjecture. What is certain is that the present pattern of in-service training neither meets the needs of education as a whole nor fulfils the rôle that the keenest young teachers expect of it.

Awareness of the failures of in-service training is by no means confined to the keenest young teachers, however. The older teacher tends to regard the system as an imposition. This view may be outdated, derived as it is from the time when in-service training for most teachers consisted of sitting in desks made for eight-year-olds at the fag-end of the day listening to second-hand advice from a speaker of probable low grade; but let's not pretend

H

that such in-service training doesn't still exist. The failure of new in-service mechanisms to get older teachers on their side itself represents a notable defeat.

At the same time, the view that in-service training has not matched up to the demands properly made upon it by curricular reform is not confined to practising teachers. The gap was charted succinctly by Brian Cane, formerly of the National Foundation for Educational Research and now deputy principal of Sheffield College of Education, in *The teacher and research* (N.F.E.R., London, 1970).

'During the last fifteen years', Cane wrote, 'major changes have been promoted in the schools to match the pace and direction of modern life. It has been too easily assumed that all that was needed to effect these changes was a reorganisation of the schools system, reform of selection and examining procedures, changes in syllabus and the introduction of new equipment. The men and women who have to put all these changes into operation have tended to be forgotten. In some sectors, notably the primary school, the demands from outside have become almost oppressive. We have been asking the front-line troops to work in new ways with new materials and new values, yet have not given them the training or the research and development support necessary.'

Brian Cane's views are reinforced by a pilot survey he conducted in four local authority areas. Cane concluded that in-service training provision was insufficient and in places patchy. His message is clear. The 'educational revolution' is a phrase which has so passed into the common usage of after-dinner speeches that we have tended to forget that a revolution is exactly what has taken place. In-service training has failed to scale up to the dimensions of subsequent changes.

Before looking more closely at this failure, it is worth examining historically the structure whose responsibility it is to retrain Britain's teachers for rôles they never suspected they might have to fill.

It has to be remembered that the philosophy of the teacher in Britain has always included a strong strain of motivation towards self-improvement. This can be traced to the class and cultural origins of teachers on which Brian Jackson and Dennis Marsden, among others, have written so perceptively, and it would be out of place to examine it in detail here. Traditionally, it has been possible to run in-service training on the cheap because teachers were prepared to go to considerable inconvenience to improve their promotion chances. Though not a restrictive device, it had the effect of confining the demand for courses to those who would make use of further training.

It was in the early 1960s that 'going on a course' changed to the more impressive concept of 'in-service training'. The new term was, in fact, coined in circumstances unlikely to win professional hearts. It was a product of the alarm of the early 1960s over the arrival of the 'second post-war bulge'. The danger level in teacher supply, which used to be seen at secondary level, suddenly swung back to the infant schools. At the same time, the increasing sophistication of official statistics revealed that large numbers of expensively trained women teachers were not repaying the cost of their qualifications before they left teaching to have children. As a result, a campaign was launched to bring experienced but lapsed women teachers back to the classroom, and the phrase 'married-women returners' was born.

This situation was loaded for existing teachers and their organisations in a number of ways. Many veteran teachers could remember the time when women teachers sent in their resignations on the same day as they put up their marriage banns. There was a good deal of feeling among older teachers, too, that colleagues who also had to cook their husbands' suppers were in some way sub-standard—regardless of the fact that many men left school at four o'clock to devote their evenings to the local cricket club, to their gardens, to masonic activities or to local politics.

A device was therefore needed to restore professional respectability to married-women returners; a device which would not, however, be a deterrent. The solution finally chosen was in-service training—which was originally, just as it sounded, training in teaching time. Married women, in the more enlightened areas anyway, brought their theory and practice up to date at courses run during normal school hours while they were paid at the appropriate Burnham rate. This was a sabbatical device which career teachers had long fought for in vain—only to see it introduced as a means of seducing back to school teachers who, in the eyes of many, were little better than deserters.

The third element in current in-service training was a spin-off from the curriculum innovation programmes sponsored first by the Nuffield Foundation and, from 1964 onwards, by the Schools Council. Even at the distance of only a handful of years, it's easy to overlook just how staggering many of the Nuffield ideas were to the majority of teachers. But to do credit to the early teams of innovators, they realised that revolutionary proposals of this magnitude could not simply be *imposed* upon teachers.

The means chosen for consultation with teachers was the teachers' centre, and from 1964 onwards these were set up in the pilot areas selected for the trials of the new Nuffield syllabuses. They were not mere training centres. They were seen as two-way establishments in which the project teams could gauge both the teaching efficiency and the teacher-acceptability of the new material they proposed to put into schools, while the teachers could both find out what was proposed and assess the proposals against real classroom situations.

The existing pattern of in-service training is thus made up of a number of disparate elements, most of which have been more in the nature of historical accidents than part of a planned policy. There are still 'refresher courses' of the old type, often run jointly by L.E.A.s and local N.U.T. associations. There are more refined variations on a similar theme, organised on a local basis by area training organisations and closely tied to initial training processes. There are local authority courses, in places still run with an eye on the married women potential but now usually broader in scope. And there are the teachers' centres.

It is evident, from the attention that they get in official circles, that it is on the teachers' centres that the educational establishment pins its hopes for a national pattern of in-service activity. 'There is some evidence', reported the Department of Education and

Science in 1970, 'that the formal course is losing some ground to the less formal meeting together of teachers . . . in teachers' centres.'

During the first three years of its life, between 1964 and 1967, the Schools Council produced no less than three working papers dealing with the development of such centres. *Working paper No. 10, Curriculum development: teachers' groups and centres,* laid down guidelines for future development. The main function of a centre, the working paper said, was 'to focus local interest and to give teachers a setting within which new objectives can be discussed and defined, and new ideas aired'. It pointed out that curriculum development required specialist accommodation, typically 'of a workshop character, combining the facilities of a demonstration laboratory with those of a practical preparation room'. The Schools Council made it clear, however, that there should be no national pattern; requirements should depend on local demand, and 'the motive power should come primarily from local groups of teachers accessible one to another'.

'It may be some time', the working paper admitted 'before the needs of teachers or the availability of funds lead local education authorities to think in terms other than encouraging the coming together of teachers in existing school buildings.'

When *Working paper No. 10* was published three years ago, there was a handful of centres in existence. Today—though the number varies according to one's definition—the list reaches well into three figures. Teachers' centres vary, however, from properly equipped and comfortably-furnished purpose-built affairs to ordinary classrooms turned over at four o'clock to the use of teachers. Organising a centre can be a full-time job for an administrator on a county inspector's salary, or a £120-a-year perk for a deputy head who has to organise local in-service training from his classroom desk in the lunch-hour. Some centres are 'workshops', whose strength is the close involvement of the grassroots teacher; others are merely lecture halls for the use of lecturers from the usual refresher-course circus who trot out for the umpteenth time their tired ideas. Some centres are run by teacher committees whose enthusiasm inspires the interest of local teachers; in others, the committee is merely a device which conceals the dead hand of the local inspectorate.

The way centres are organised is only one critical factor of success. Another—probably even more vital—is the extent to which L.E.A. policy permits them to be used during the day. *Working paper No. 10* noted that 'regular evening and weekend use should develop quickly, but day use from Monday to Friday will depend on the policies, particularly those of staffing, of individual authorities'.

That teachers have firm views on when they should go to the centres was indicated by a survey of attitudes to in-service training conducted among some 10,000 teachers for the D.E.S. and published as *Statistics of Education SS2: Survey of in-service training for teachers* in 1970. This showed that: 'The time when teachers wish to make use of a teachers' centre appears to be mainly in school hours, immediately after school, or in the evenings of school days'. Only a quarter of the teachers in the survey wanted to use a centre at weekends, and only a third during the school holidays.

On the question of *when* in-service training is best conducted, teachers are more in agreement than on the question of *where*. Teachers were asked when they would prefer to attend residential courses. 'The use of school hours,' the D.E.S. noted primly, 'was the only suggestion which met with greater approval than disapproval.'

It is not surprising that teachers are reluctant to pay for their own increased efficiency by working in their spare time. They have been told often enough that one of the reasons why teachers' pay is not higher is because they have a short working day and long holidays. They know, too, that in-service training in other fields of employment—the banks, commerce and industry, the civil service—is conducted in working time, generally in more comfortable circumstances, and often directly related to promotion. Teachers are not so short of ways of filling their spare time as to need to spend it in substandard conditions reminiscent of the Victorian parish reading.

This point was effectively made to me by a primary school

teacher, whose neighbour, also in his mid-forties, had been trained as a hot-metal compositor and had spent all his working life on the local weekly paper. Then his employers had decided to convert to film-setting, and the compositor had had to settle down in mid-career and learn his job all over again.

'So they gave him a crash course in film-setting,' the teacher told me, 'and then let him finish off his retraining on the job. And when he'd finished, and he'd mastered his new skills, he got a proficiency bonus. Catch that happening in teaching! Take this course I'm on.

'I take the car, but apparently my local authority doesn't believe in teachers riding in cars because all I can claim back is the bus fare. So I rush home at four o'clock and grab some tea, and off I go to the course. By the time it ends and I've had a drink with the others, it's half past eight, so I either have to buy a meal out or have my supper heated up when I get home. I can't claim for a meal, of course; my local authority doesn't believe in teachers eating, either, it seems. So I've missed my favourite television programme and I'll have to get to school early the next day to finish my marking—and for what? I suppose it's something to put on my next application form, but that's about all.'

Several teachers I spoke to had serious doubts about the value of the in-service training they had undertaken, even with the strictly limited objective of helping them to do their day-to-day work better. There were complaints about tired ideas, incompetent or ill-informed speakers, and the constant re-tilling of well-ploughed ground. 'If I hear any more about Piaget, I'll walk out,' threatened one veteran course attender.

Another teacher suspected that some trivial or frivolous courses were devised in order to fill up in-service programmes. He had been invited by a local adviser to sign up for a weekend on classroom display. His reply had been that he had no wish to spend a weekend learning how to use drawing-pins and Sellotape, and this was not well received. The same teacher told me that it seemed that in his area it didn't matter much what course you went on, as long as you went. He had applied for a primary school English course, and had been told that the places were all taken, but he could go on an art and craft weekend instead.

Married-women teachers, often under particular pressure to attend for in-service training, are particularly sensitive about the difficulties involved in the present system. One told me about the interview for her present job at which 'the man from the office' had asked if she'd been on any courses lately. She had explained that with a husband and two children to look after it wasn't easy to make arrangements. The man from the office sniffed contemptuously, 'and I thought I'd had it'. She hadn't though; he was merely exercising the time-honoured right of members of interviewing panels to be bloody to interviewees.

This teacher made the further point, though, that attendance at courses isn't everything. Following the educational news in a national paper, plus the weekly reading of a teachers' journal, and subscribing to an educational monthly, she felt she was pretty well informed about current trends. 'But you can't send in a copy of your newsagent's bill with your application form—and you can't claim the money back from the office, either.'

Money, time, recognition: these seem to be the rocks upon which in-service training, from the teachers' point of view, presently founders. They feel that the total cost of in-service training should be refunded by their L.E.A.s; they feel that training should take place in their employers' time; and they feel that it should be recognised.

In the D.E.S. survey it was noted that 'The suggestions of rewarding course attendance through the Burnham salary scale or through promotion attracted considerable support.' It was, perhaps, unfair of the survey team to put this idea into respondents' minds, because the need for in-service training is most marked among the unambitious teacher who is least likely to be seduced by financial blandishments. The problem of 'recognition' is the most intractable one. In any case, is mere attendance at a course enough? Is it really better to have attended and let every word pass over your head than never to have attended at all?

A way of organising in-service training more effectively and

fairly is not too difficult to devise, and I outline here some proposals which received almost unanimous support from my sample
of teachers. The proposals came from teachers themselves. After
writing a series of articles touching upon some of the problems
of in-service training, I received a number of letters nearly all of
which called for the same thing: a national scheme under which
x days per year should be set aside for teacher re-education.
Here are my proposals.

It seems to me that, at a time of tremendous educational
change, the educational establishment cannot ignore its obligation
to provide some better pattern of re-training than the present
shakedown system. It must also be accepted that the new pattern
will cost a fair amount of employers' money. I would therefore
first make an analysis of which in-service needs could be met in
teachers' centres and which called for residential courses of
varying lengths. This in itself would cut out a lot of wasteful
duplication.

Turning first to teachers' centres, each local authority should
be asked to prepare for the D.E.S.'s approval a detailed plan for
equipping its area with an adequate number of centres, which
should ideally be purpose-built. A minimum cost per place
should be laid down for building and equipment, and this sum
should be high enough to avoid substandard decoration, provision
or furnishing. Teachers should not be expected to take on the
work of making their centre habitable as if it were a youth club
or some other worthy voluntary cause.

There should also be a minimum annual budget for running
expenses which would include such items as the cost of a tea-lady
and washers-up; teachers at most centres have to take part in
do-it-yourself refreshments. A standard for reference facilities
should be established and adhered to, and wardens of centres
should not have to depend on charity, the goodwill of the office,
or commercial handouts for providing exhibitions of current
teaching aids, books and materials. Local authorities should
receive guidance on the staffing of centres, which should be run
by full-time wardens—preferably recruited from the classroom
rather than from the office—paid appropriately for the job.

The use of teachers' centres outside school hours—at least so far as in-service training is concerned, though they might profitably be used for other purposes such as general adult education—should be exceptional rather than commonplace. Local authorities should be expected to maintain staffing standards which would permit an agreed minimum of attendance by each teacher—perhaps the equivalent of five days per term. Head teachers should be responsible for seeing that staff were released without difficulty; the problem of finding a replacement and dislike of giving colleagues extra work were among leading factors weighing heavily against course attendance according to the D.E.S. survey.

Similarly exact provision should be made for course attendance other than at teachers' centres. It should be possible to write into teachers' contracts the condition that of the 200 days a year a teacher is normally expected to work at least five (say) should be on courses. (If the teacher attended weekend or holiday courses, he should be entitled to take teaching days off *in lieu*.) To develop the system still further, each course could be given a points rating, with each teacher required to notch up a given number of points during the year.

It would go without saying that *all* expenses incurred in in-service training (and this would include baby-sitters, if necessary, for married women teachers) would be repayable by the local authorities.

Other contributions to this book, and most contributions to the wider debate on teacher education, are much concerned with *where* problems, and I should possibly conclude with something about who should direct this national pattern of in-service training. I must admit that I can see no perfect answer to this. It seems to me that on the record of the colleges of education, they are least well equipped, and likely to remain so, to become involved with a scheme which must essentially be rooted in classroom experience. But clearly a national scheme would be too big to entrust to local authorities. I would be tempted to suggest a solution along the lines of the Schools Council, a National In-Service Training Authority, if only the teachers' organisations could be restrained from turning it into another arena for their internecine disputes. Perhaps, as a result of whatever changes take place in the organisation of initial teacher training, a possible structure will become visible.

This much is certain: structure is, above all, what in-service training needs.

15 Teaching the teachers

Bruce Kemble

Inquiries into teacher training have usually concentrated on *where* the training takes place. Detailed, lengthy debates have been carried on about the status of the colleges providing the courses. We are, in our investigation, more interested in 'Who?', or 'What?' questions, than in this question of 'Where?'

We want to examine ways of improving the quality of the students, and the trainers. We are worried about who teaches what to whom. Other contributors, notably Michael Storm, have dealt with the reforms needed in the courses. Nicholas Bagnall has, in the final section, outlined our positive suggestions for the improvement of training. It is my task to place the production of teachers in the context of our divisive, and wasteful, education system.

But so much has been said, and written, about the proper *place* of training, it is necessary to deal with some of the key points in this debate. Whoever makes the final decisions about the future structure of higher education will need to be aware of some of the qualifications and counter-arguments in this controversy. Some say teachers ought to be trained in the polytechnics, others advocate new liberal arts colleges, others urge stronger links between the colleges of education and the universities, and a few talk hopefully, and vaguely, about 'comprehensive universities'.

Supporters of the polytechnics accuse the colleges of education of being 'monotechnics'. They admire the vocational traditions of the polys, and say teacher training belongs with them, rather than in the academic tradition of the universities. They add that teachers would benefit from studying alongside students on other courses. Opponents of this view deny the colleges are narrow. The Association of Education Committees, for example, say: 'The range of subjects necessarily involved in a college of education is extremely wide; indeed it is probably wider than in other establishments of higher education which would not be regarded as "monotechnic".'

Stanley Hewett, general secretary of the A.T.C.D.E., has made a vigorous defence of the colleges, and scored some hits. He scorns the idea that membership of a polytechnic will break down the 'isolation' of a college of education. Some colleges would still be 30 or 40 miles away from their parent poly, he points out. Mr Hewett also claims that, in the seven polys which have education departments, the 'dream of intending teachers working alongside those preparing for other careers is not realised'. He say: 'In one poly, at least, the students, in certain subjects, have to go to the nearby college of education, for part of their fourth-year course, as the poly *cannot provide* the necessary teaching. Their students do, however, have the right to queue alongside the remainder of students for cafeteria services.'

His solution is for the colleges to become part of a network of university-dominated higher education institutions. But in view of all the valid criticism of the way the universities have handled teacher training in general, and the B.Ed. in particular, few educationists will warm to this suggestion.

Meanwhile Dr Eric Midwinter, Keith Gardner and others back the notion of a 'socially inter-professional college where all students, with some social commitment, and a fancy for teaching, nursery welfare, probation, etc., might do a foundation course from which they might choose their later specialism'. The main objection to this is that the number of teachers in such a college will always so outweigh the other students there will be little or no benefit to the would-be teachers. Critics of this proposal point out that the young teachers might as well have stayed in the colleges of education. Michael Storm says that in such a college the non-teachers would be merely used as 'visual aids'.

Mr Hewett's remark about students only meeting those on other courses in the cafeteria applies equally well to students on most university courses at present. It is a debating point which does not remove the objections to the present system of training— which are outlined so vividly in Richard Bourne's and Nicholas Bagnall's chapters.

The advocates of a 'comprehensive university' must be clearer about the nuts and bolts of their theories, before we can accept them as a coherent alternative to the present set-up. They must be more realistic about the prejudices of our status-crazy society and the higher education power game.

Two points must be made, however, about the future of universities. Countries such as Denmark, Belgium, France and America have begun turning their efforts to developing non-university institutions. This has not escaped the notice of senior experts at the Department of Education and Science. One told me: 'About 90 per cent of the students at universities are exposed at the undergraduate level to a course beautifully adapted to produce future dons. But the vast majority are not going to be dons.' The Tory Government from the moment of its election in 1970 showed a strong distaste for university expansion, and a liking for the polytechnics.

Secondly, it is important for those who think we can solve social-class friction by tinkering with the titles of educational institutions to remember another comment by the same man. He said: 'There is no reason to think if a future plumber were to receive his higher education side by side with a future surgeon they would both enjoy the same status in society on that account.' Sooner or later we are going to have to decide why we reward physical strength less than brain power, but we do, and we are likely to do so in an unjust, and illogical, way for a long time to come. It would seem to be a start, however, to ensure that future plumbers and surgeons got more opportunities to study together.

But when we have admitted that the 'comprehensive university' is not a clear proposal, when we have rejected part of the arguments put forward by supporters of liberal arts colleges, or the polys, we still have to face the evidence which exposes the inadequacy of the present training system. The case against the colleges is proved.

One experienced supporter of the colleges wrote to me recently: 'I get rather apoplectic when the incessant radical reappraisers feel no obligation to look at all closely at what is actually going on in the colleges—being so convinced that whatever it is is wrong. Indeed a case could be made out that the colleges' greatest problems spring, not from an inert traditionalism, but from a breathless and naïve willingness to respond to every pressure, every recommendation, from every side, simultaneously!' This book is my reply to this letter. We have looked at the colleges. We have spoken to practising teachers, and given them a chance to report on how their training prepared them for the classroom. We have looked at the students in the colleges. These students (see the Bourne and Bagnall chapters) have first-hand experience of 'what is going on in the colleges'. Their evidence must not be ignored. As a result of our research we agree with the spirit of some comments from Graham Owens, Head of the Department of Education, Trent Polytechnic, who said: 'The colleges have shown themselves largely *irrelevant* to the needs of the contemporary system.'

But one point must be made in defence of the colleges at this stage. Many of their critics are worried because there is tension between the colleges and the schools. They are upset because progressive-minded, idealistic teachers are in conflict with conservative colleagues in the staff-room. They complain that this shows how out-of-touch the colleges are. They urge veteran teachers to get into the colleges to tell the woolly-minded staff what the classroom coal-face is like. There is some truth in these exaggerations, but it must be said that *any* healthy training system would be in conflict with the schools. Students by definition should be trained in an inquiring atmosphere favourable to radical ideas. It is essential that they do come into a school eager to convert the lazy, the reactionary and the ignorant. Many will always succumb to the first old sweat who advises: 'You can forget all the nonsense they told you in college.' But some will leave that school a better, happier and more self-critical place than they found it.

One obvious way in which students in the future are going to clash with older colleagues is over their differing attitudes to parents and pupils. Senior teachers and heads will find it hard in many cases to appreciate the 'democratic' outlook of the young teachers straight from college. This book welcomes the spread of 'community' schools which encourage this approach. Schools such as Tattenhall Primary in Cheshire, or the new Isle of Sheppey Comprehensive are good examples of institutions which welcome parents, and recognise the rôle of a school in its local setting. Other 'community schools' can be found in Cumberland, Cambridgeshire, Leicestershire and Nottinghamshire. These schools surprise those parents and teachers who believe nothing is valuable unless it is painfully acquired. They are places which remind us of the original meaning of the word 'school'—a place for 'worthwhile leisure'. Just as our uneducated society in the mediaeval period was unified by the Church, so our semi-educated community could be unified by such schools when they are part of a system of education. Such schools (co-educational, comprehensive, unstreamed, day schools) would be thought of by pupils, parents and local citizens as 'our school'. We must stop the nonsense of allowing head teachers to get away with talking about 'my school'. It never has been his, or her, school in any healthy or meaningful sense.

Other developments in education give hope that our school/college network will get more unified. The Educational Priority Areas, especially those in Liverpool and Deptford, the tendency of authorities, such as Exeter and Barnstaple, to co-ordinate provision for teenagers in schools and technical colleges, and the move in Loughborough to increase co-operation between post-school colleges and the universities—all these give grounds for optimism that education will become better organised.

We commend the attitude of the U.N.E.S.C.O. pamphlet published in May 1971 which outlined a vision of an education system quite foreign to the minds who created our method of 'schooling apartheid', which sends 30,000 bright teenagers every year off to manual jobs, and which produces 286,000 school-leavers totally unequipped to cope with the world outside the classroom, and often barely literate. The U.N.E.S.C.O. document said: 'The ideal would be a system of educational services available to people of all ages, ranging from the cradle to the grave. These would be arranged for the convenience of all age groups, and the content would be such as to cater for all interests and learning styles and speeds. . . . There would be no failures in such a system. It would be geared to helping people explore their own skills . . . at their own pace . . . none would be ostracised for not maturing *all* their interests when in formal school as children.'

A schooling system based on such a liberated approach with real contacts with the local community, would produce more mature and inquisitive applicants for teacher training. At present, as the research in our first chapter shows, the applicants are uncurious and immature. They come from grammar schools which are designed to protect, and isolate, pupils from both the world outside the classroom, and the fruits of meaningful inquiry.

Just as these new 'community' schools are smashing the artificial barriers erected by our class-conscious society, so post-school education should be encouraged to develop along the same lines. Cities such as Manchester, or Cardiff, could immediately examine ways of copying the co-ordination and co-operation evident between colleges in Loughborough. This would be a start.

But one objection is always raised when anyone suggests that student teachers should come into closer contact with the future parents of their pupils. It is said that putting student teachers in the same student union, or cafeteria, as students on other courses, would have a disastrous effect on teacher supply. We are told that the commitment of the average student is so feeble that a brief chat with an apprentice printer, on the verge of a £40-a-week job, would deprive our classrooms of another 'Mr Chips'. My reaction to this may seem unrealistic, but I am not alarmed by these fears. It seems that if a teacher can be so easily seduced away from a job he is no great loss to the classroom. It seems to me that it is up to the Government to use its considerable resources to mount a counter-offensive to the case put by apprentice printers. They could start paying teachers properly. They might consider a campaign to promote the cause of teachers among the ratepayers. They could recognise the value of a profession full of people who *earn* money rather than 'make' it. Allowing teachers to train alongside students on other courses could put more money in their pockets, and give them more status and self-respect.

Many of the participants in the big debate over the best way to educate and train teachers have neglected to deal with this problem of supply. The A.E.C. say quite blandly that after the school leaving-age has been raised we must prepare to *reduce* the supply of teachers which is increasing at the rate of 18,000 a year. Other groups and some politicians have sung the same complacent song. It is necessary to point out that at the last count over 1,280,000 secondary school children were in classes over-30, and 429,000 pupils in primary schools were handicapped by having more than 40 classmates. It is folly to talk of cutting the supply until there is not a single class with more than 30 children.

It is necessary, whatever network of colleges is arranged to produce the teachers, for a new body to be set up to supervise the training standards and the output of teachers. We do not want a body like the old National Advisory Council, disbanded by Mr Crosland, and we do not need a Teachers' Council. Squabbling teacher politicians do not make sound administrators, or wise judges, or objective leaders. It should not, however, be difficult for a Government to appoint a body peopled by the sort of men and women who are persuaded to serve on a Central Advisory Council.

This body would have enormous influence on every aspect of education. All educational problems are umbilically-linked to the question: 'How can we produce better teachers?' We hope that such a body would agree with us when we say we produced this book because we believe a concentration on teacher education/training is the most direct way of jacking up standards throughout the *whole* school-college set-up.

We also believe certain efforts should be made at other key points in the education to ensure the supply of better, happier candidates for training. We do not need to stress the benefits of providing a nursery school place for every child aged three to five. We hardly have to remind you that parents are the teenagers of yesterday, and therefore at some point in our education system we need to equip them with the knowledge, and experience, to enable them to be better parents. We need parents who talk, and *listen,* to their children. We also need to abolish streaming in primary schools, and the remaining selective secondary schools, which have such a harmful effect on the primary, and comprehensive, schools in their area.

These efforts, along with the reforms mentioned earlier, would give us an education system more likely to produce student teachers of a higher quality.

Our suggestions are not entirely original, but, if they were adopted in conjunction with the reforms of schools (especially the unstreaming of primary schools, and the reorganisation of secondary schools) they would be revolutionary. We are not rejecting other similar recommendations entirely. For example we urge the decision-makers to look closely at the Nottingham 'module' which is related to the idea of the 'teacher/advisor' or 'teacher/tutor' who helps the student on school practice. Graham Owens at Trent Polytechnic has devised a 'module', or a unit, of 70-odd students with about six tutors. They work more closely together than is usual. Although it is a small unit it is not a closed, claustrophobic group. Other teachers, some social workers, other professional and lay people, are involved whenever they are needed. College, students, pupils and school are closely involved in the local community. He says: 'It can form the basic unit of school, college, polytechnic, university, institute of education, teachers' centre, community workshop . . . It provides the basis for an educated, . . . democratic community.'

Graham Owens' work, and the H.M.A. recommendations for teacher/tutors, depend of course on there being an adequate supply of good teachers available to supervise the students in schools. It is quite clear that there are not enough good teachers

to go round. Professor Evans (who would be expected to put a
favourable interpretation on his experience in the colleges as
their former spokesman) admits that only one teacher in
six could be called 'good'. Unfortunately these men and
women are not spread evenly throughout the country's 28,000
schools. It is also worth remembering when one is urging the
idea of teacher/tutors that (according to the D.E.S.) *all* schools are
used at some time during a five-year period for practice. Some
schools do not have a teacher able, or willing, to perform the
rôle of mentor. But these qualifications do not alter our admira-
tion of Mr Owens' achievement.

We commend the approach of such men. Although it is hard
to be precise about the best ways of 'giving education back to
the people', or of making schools 'more democratic', it is clear
that such sentiments cannot be expressed too often. Our vision
of the education system of the future contains a view of students
leaving schools where they were made aware there is a great
variety of social classes (and an opposite sex). Far too many of
our schools are one social-class, single-sex schools producing
'socially handicapped' children. The schools in our vision should
appeal to future Socialist, and Tory, Ministers. They should
appeal to Socialist ideals of equality of opportunity. They
should be attractive to those who believe, in the words of the
late Iain Macleod, 'children should have an equal chance to be
unequal'. They must surely appeal to the Tories who will
find our praise of 'community schools', and our breaking down
of barriers in higher education, a sound, human way of creating
One Nation'.

A summary of recommendations for the reform of teacher training

This book has shown that there is a great deal wrong with our way of training teachers. But identifying a problem is not quite the same as solving it. Pious or declaratory aspirations are not much help. We have tried to avoid them here. For example, to recommend that 'there should be closer liaison between the colleges of education and the practice schools' is not really to make a recommendation at all; it is simply another way of saying that there is not enough liaison now. It does nothing to put the matter right.

The recommendations below are all designed to bring us nearer a situation in which (a) the education service gets its fair share of people with quality and talent, and (b) their training is relevant to the needs of the schools.

1. Entry qualifications

Requirements for entry to a teacher training course must be on a par with those for university or for a degree course in a polytechnic. This is not to say that the two-A-level requirement is the right one; but there must be parity. The recommendation is made with reluctance—partly because of the very imperfect correlations between A-level grades and college performance, partly because of the large numbers of students without any A levels who later go on to be successful teachers. But against their possible loss we must measure a possible gain in the numbers of good A-levellers who might well have gone in for teaching but for the colleges' low esteem in the minds of teachers and parents. The remedy is crude, but the clearing-house figures show that it is necessary.

2. *Final qualification*

For precisely the same reason, all teacher training courses leading to qualified-teacher status should confer a degree.

3. *Consecutive or concurrent?*

We must reject the 'concurrent' concept of training. In principle it aims to marry theory and practice, but it has manifestly failed to do so. Instead, it has merely produced a jigsaw of bits and pieces whose connections students often find it hard to understand; the approach to the individual parts may be perfunctory, yet the total syllabus is exhausting. It also has the disadvantage of assuming a commitment to teach which cannot always be expected of 18-year-olds.

What we must seek is a formula which recognises:

(a) that some students, though not necessarily particularly brilliant, can achieve academic rigour through the excitement of wanting to teach (which the traditional 'main subject' does not give them);

(b) that for others, the reverse process may apply;

(c) that for both categories, close and extended contact with children *and* their families is essential if students are to bring understanding to their professional studies, and that this experience needs to come at the point at which commitment is clear.

No single formula can be expected to cope adequately with all these three—the first two, for example, would seem to call for contrary solutions. The best pattern, in practice, would be:

(i) A two-year academic course, not necessarily committed to teaching, but incorporating education as an element, whether 'major' or 'minor', and leading to

(ii) EITHER (a) a third academic year, leading to a degree, for those who do not want to teach but are good enough to take a conventional B.A.,

OR (b) a year of practical training for those who do want to teach, followed by

(iii) a year of education theory for those who have successfully completed their practical year.

The practical year should see the student engaged as an active and accepted member of a school staff, working as an aide, not unlike the medical student attached to a hospital, with tutors exercising the same oversight as hospital consultants exercise over medicos. The year should include social work, home visiting and the study of individual children, which would be of vital use to the schools as well as to the students.

4. *Length of course*

It follows from the above that the normal teacher training course should last four years.

5. *Differential training*

We must repudiate the assumption, made by teachers' organisations, that there is a single quality—'the ability to teach'—which is common to all members of the profession wherever they may practise. We must recognise that the qualities needed for an infant teacher may be different from (though not inferior to) those needed for a sixth-form teacher.

We see some teachers taking a four-year course as sketched out above, others taking professional training after a three-year degree, others a professional C.N.A.A. degree in a polytechnic, particularly suitable for category (a) in paragraph 3 above. (In the latter connection, we would commend the 'module' system as seen in, for example, Trent Polytechnic for close attention.) It is worth asking, however, whether entry into the profession through the degree-plus-diploma system should qualify for teaching in all types of school. We would certainly regard this as an inadequate training for teaching in primary schools, and probably for teaching in unselective secondary schools as well. In any case, the probationary year should still be required for those who choose to do the one-year post-graduate course. For those who have come up through the route outlined in (3) above, probation would not be necessary.

6. *Structure of the colleges*

These recommendations assume the disappearance of the college of education sector as a separate entity. Some could become schools of the relevant university—they could be absorbed, in short, into the university itself; others could attach themselves to a polytechnic; others, again, could become polytechnics in their own right. Some which are too small or remote to be viable could become important teachers' centres and play a vital part in in-service training, particularly of older teachers, which we believe should be compulsory.

Easy transfer between one type of institution and another is essential. For example, a student could start his academic career in a college and continue it in a university or in a polytechnic; or vice versa. We regard the 'comprehensive university' concept as lacking in definition, but believe that experiments like those proposed at Loughborough should be watched with interest.

The 'liberal arts college' proposal does not, we believe, go far enough in the direction we are suggesting, and would leave the colleges largely monotechnic, which is generally agreed to be a disadvantage.

7. *A credit system*

Ease of transfer between institutions implies a credit system. It would be up to university faculties, for example, to decide how many credits in a particular subject (or branch of a subject) a student at the end of his second year would need so as to qualify for exemption from the first part of a degree course. Such a system should also be used to ensure that freshly trained teachers do not teach in schools for which their training has not suited them (see paragraph 5 above). Thus no teacher would be able to teach in a primary school unless he had collected the requisite credit in the teaching of reading, or in a school with a high proportion of immigrants without a credit in the teaching of English as a second language. (Since we would propose that

regular secondment for in-service training should be compulsory, an in-service teacher who wanted to teach in a different kind of school would have the opportunity of picking up the necessary extra credit.)

8. A national body

At present the academic standards of the colleges of education are ensured through the university institutes under the system of Area Training Organisations. In a 'diversified' pattern of colleges such as has been proposed here, this could no longer be so. This need not be regretted, since it is one of the themes of this book that the colleges have been too closely in the grip of the universities, whose views of what qualifications a teacher ought to have are not always relevant to the needs either of the teachers themselves or of the schools. At the same time, we are under the obvious charge of wanting the best of two worlds: of asking for academic respectability (degree status for all future teachers) and of insisting on a more vocational bias for trainees. The two need not, however, be incompatible: the C.N.A.A. system has enabled them to be reconciled in the polytechnics.

A national course-approving body like the C.N.A.A. would not be appropriate for the colleges, if only because there are five times as many of them as there are polytechnics. The machine would be too unwieldy. There would need, in fact, to be two kinds of body: (a) a national body, exercising the functions of the old National Advisory Council on the Training and Supply of Teachers, which would advise the Government on the supply position and would also lay down general standards; and (b) a number of regional advisory councils which would approve individual courses. We would expect (a) to include representatives both of the local education authorities, as employers, and also of the universities, as well as of the professional associations. Similarly, (b) would represent all the academic interests involved.

Of course the administrative problems are not as simple as this. In particular, the initial two-year course proposed in paragraph 3 presents obvious difficulties. The course is seen as having four functions:

As an initial course for intending teachers;
as an initial course for students who are aiming for a degree
    but not to teach;
as a terminal course for other professions; and
as a terminal course for students not wishing further education
    or training.

While no one particularly wants a proliferation of councils
and committees, the idea of an H.E.D., or Higher Education
Diploma, for this course, with or without its own examining
board, is highly tempting. It would be regrettable if the universities did not also allow their students to go for the H.E.D. (or
whatever it might be called); and a suitable system of credits,
or exemptions, should not be beyond the wit of academic man.

9. A staff college

The 'practical year' also needs some careful working out. To put
the practical training of students entirely into the hands of school
staffs would be regarded by many as a retrogressive step, and
would be strongly resisted by the colleges. On the other hand,
many college tutors are at present not properly qualified to
supervise teaching practice, and there is resentment among some
schools because of this. We would regard the practical year as
the joint responsibility of tutors and of chosen teachers. A college
for training tutors in teaching, attendance at which would
qualify a college lecturer to supervise trainees in class, would do
much to restore confidence between the two groups.

By no means all these recommendations are approved by
everyone who has contributed to this book—that would be too
much to ask. But all of us would agree with their aims and spirit.

Notes on contributors

NICHOLAS BAGNALL, 46, has been education correspondent of the *Sunday Telegraph* since 1965. Before that he was for four years editor of the National Union of Teachers' journal, *The Teacher,* which was called the *Schoolmaster and Woman Teacher's Chronicle* before he took it over and transformed it into a weekly educational newspaper in its own right.

He first came to Fleet Street in 1953 as a sub-editor on the *Daily Telegraph,* writing feature articles in his spare time. His first article on education appeared in the *Telegraph* in 1954, and a natural interest in the subject, stemming from his experience as a part-time teacher some eight years earlier, gradually grew till by 1960 he was spending more than half his time writing on the subject.

He was educated at Bryanston and at Wadham College, Oxford, where he read Classical Mods and English. Has a wife who is a teacher.

RICHARD BOURNE, 31, educated at Uppingham School, took a modern history degree at Brasenose College, Oxford, and joined the *Guardian* as a trainee reporter in Manchester in 1962. With the exception of six months' leave of absence on a Brazilian Government scholarship in Brazil in 1965 he has worked in several capacities as a *Guardian* journalist since then. Since February 1968 he has been the paper's education correspondent. Has written: *Political Leaders of Latin America* and is joint author, with Brian

MacArthur, of the official history of the National Union of Teachers, *Struggle for Education, 1870–1970.*

RONALD DEADMAN, formerly features editor of *The Teacher,* an editor of *Everyweek,* is now editor of *Teacher's World* and a member of the Press Council. He has taught in primary and secondary schools, worked with adult immigrants in an evening institute, and with day-release students in further education, and has lectured in a college of education. He taught for one year in the United States as an 'exchange' teacher.

He has written four textbooks in English, two science-fiction books for 8–11-year-olds, edited an anthology of short stories for juniors, and contributed to the *New Statesman,* the *Guardian,* the B.B.C. (short stories and contributions to further education programmes), *Where* magazine, *Education and Training* and *Art and Craft in Education.*

ALEX EVANS, 56, attended elementary school and Queen Elizabeth's Hospital, Bristol. He spent twenty years in classrooms in Portsmouth and Middlesex, and at Bedales School. He was successively an H.M.I., Deputy Director of the University of Leeds Institute of Education, Principal of the College of St Mark and St John, Chelsea, and General Secretary of the Association of Teachers in Colleges and Departments of Education. He 'retired' in 1970, but is Director and Professor of Literature, London Centre for English Studies, Antioch College, Ohio. Has lectured in Germany, Hungary, Turkey, and edited Shakespeare's plays and various anthologies. Has visited, and examined in, over a hundred colleges of education.

JOHN EZARD, 31, is on the *Guardian's* education staff. Now the only non-State schoolteacher in his family, he was educated at two public schools in Devon and Essex, 'which gave me a lifelong interest in any attempts to produce an alternative, rational system of discipline'. He later read English at St Catherine's College, Cambridge. He joined the *Guardian* after spells as education reporter and university correspondent of the *Oxford Mail.*

DAVID FLETCHER, 32, covers education for the *Daily Telegraph* and has written extensively about teachers and students in national, provincial and evening newspapers for more than ten years. His wife is at present a student at a college of education, and both their children are at primary school.

KEITH GARDNER, is a lecturer at the School of Education, University of Nottingham, where he is responsible for Advanced Diploma work with primary school teachers. He is also actively engaged on in-service courses for serving teachers. He has had over twenty years' experience as a teacher in primary and special education. His main interest has been the teaching of reading, in which field he is a recognised authority. He is a frequent contributor to educational discussion both in print and on television.

BRUCE KEMBLE, 33, has been education reporter of the *Daily Express* for the past six years, after working on a news agency and for the B.B.C. He is a Cambridge graduate.

This is the fourth book he has been associated with. For *Looking Forward to the 70's* he wrote the longest chapter—an attack on streaming called 'Condemned at Seven' which aroused a great deal of interest in the educational world.

He was also the inspiration behind a book called *Crisis in the Classroom,* which attempted to alert parents and politicians to the dangers of the Labour Government's policy of curbing the expansion of educational expenditure.

His last book, *Give Your Child a Chance,* was biased in favour of parents. It established him as a 'one-man advisory centre for education', helping the 10 million readers of his newspaper with their educational problems.

ERIC MIDWINTER, 39, Mancunian, read History at Cambridge and took a D.Phil. at York. His career has been mostly in colleges of education. At present he is Director of the Liverpool Priority Area Project and Co-Director of the Advisory Centre of Education, Cambridge. In 1972 he becomes Director of Priority, a national centre in Liverpool for E.P.A. and allied work. Author of five books and of many articles and papers on the education of the socially disadvantaged, notably *Education: a Priority Area* (N.U.T. booklet).

MAUREEN O'CONNOR, 31, freelance journalist and broadcaster, was educated at Bradford Girls' Grammar School and Birmingham University (B.A., English). She served as a reporter on the *Yorkshire Post*, the *Guardian* and the *Evening Standard*. She taught, briefly, in a girls' secondary modern school in the West Country, and was the Deputy Editor of *The Teacher* for two years, then a reporter and producer with B.B.C. radio. Since 1969 has been freelancing, writing for the *Guardian*, *Education and Training* and other educational papers, and broadcasting mainly on education. Has written a cookery book for children.

GORDON PEMBERTON, born in Liverpool in 1919 of Irish extraction, survived a conventional lower-middle-class upbringing and education. He entered training college (Chester) in 1938 and the following autumn began six war years in the Army, which completely changed his attitude to life. In 1946 he finished his training and emerged from college with distinction and a burning zeal which has never left him. Six years in the Liverpool slums and twelve in the industrial West Riding gave him a wealth of experience, an urge for progress and an impolite contempt for educational privilege. For his third headship, in 1964, he opened Broadlands School, Hereford, where he first practises what he later preaches. Teacher, lecturer, author, atheist and anti-establishment rebel, he enjoys trailing his coat all over traditional education.

MICHAEL POLLARD was a teacher for ten years before turning to full-time writing on education. He has been, in succession, features editor of *The Teacher*, editor of *Read*, deputy editor of *Teacher's World* and editor of *Pictorial Education*; he is also a prolific contributor on educational topics to a number of national magazines and newspapers. His books include schoolbooks for both primary and secondary levels, and an A-to-Z guide to education for parents, *Education today and how it works.*

Currently, Michael Pollard edits a new monthly journal for teachers, *Resources*, which aims to fill what he believes is a serious communications gap between those responsible for innovation and change and the classroom teacher who has to carry new ideas into practice.

MICHAEL STORM, 36, a geography graduate who taught in Hull, Leeds and Manchester before taking up his present post as principal lecturer and head of the Geography Department at the Berkshire College of Education. His special interests are in urban studies, Third World studies, and the development of geographical skills and concepts in young children. He has published a book on urban problems for secondary schools, and one on maps for infants. He regularly contributes articles and reviews to *Teacher's World* and other educational journals. He spent 1967-8 on secondment to the Cyprus Ministry of Education, working on curriculum development in environmental studies, and has taken part in in-service training courses in West Africa and Jamaica.

SHIRLEY TOULSON, editor of the monthly journal *Child Education*, and formerly features editor of *The Teacher*, has been connected with educational journalism since 1958 when she joined the staff of *Visual Education*. Before that she taught for four years, having taken a degree in English at Birkbeck College and the Postgraduate Certificate in Education at the London University Institute of Education. She has three children, one of whom is just completing his postgraduate year at the Centre for Science Education.

FRANCES VERRINDER, 28, went to nine schools (including a pit-village primary, a conventual public day girls' school in

Birmingham and a trendy West London comprehensive) and was thus convinced at an early age that the education system was badly in need of reform. After university, teaching and the civil service, she went into educational publishing and from there into journalism. She has written for a number of educational journals and is currently editor of the new monthly, *Drugs and Society*.